KNITTED SWEATER

STYLE

KNITTED SWEATER
STYLE

INSPIRATIONS IN
COLOR

JO SHARP

The Taunton Press

Taunton
BOOKS & VIDEOS
for fellow enthusiasts

First printing: 1997
Printed in the United States of America

A THREADS Book
THREADS® is a trademark of The Taunton Press, Inc.,
registered in the U.S. Patent and Trademark Office.

The Taunton Press, 63 South Main Street, Box 5506,
Newtown, CT 06470-5506

Library of Congress Cataloging-in-Publication Data
Sharp, Jo.
        Knitted sweater style : inspirations in color / Jo Sharp.
            p. cm.
        ISBN 1-56158-189-5
        1. Knitting—Patterns. 2. Sweaters. I. Title.
TT825.S49 1997
746.43'20432—dc20   96-41737
                                                  CIP

CONTENTS

ACKNOWLEDGMENTS

Coordination & Styling:
Jenni Holmes, Ricarda Loecker,
Wendy Richards

Photographers: Warren Bellette,
Jo Sharp

Models: David Bayley, Wendy Cullen,
Loren Dean, Jessica Dyer,
Nicole Edwards, Phaedra Golebiowski,
Jenni Holmes, Drew Lange,
Ella Macdonald, Jack Markovs,
Rita Sophia Markovs, David Rhia,
Timothy Sharp, Nicole Spanbroek,
Tammy Toovey, Jody Tovey, Leah York,
Steve York

Makeup: Loren Dean, Sarah Elliot,
Linda Trewern

Hair: Dateline Hair Design

Technical Assistants: Elaine Reynolds,
Bronia Richards

Pattern Assistants: Sonia Charewicz,
Jennifer Green, Debra Kinsey,
Wendy Richards, Coby Yzerman

INTRODUCTION

I HAVE COME TO REALIZE THAT COLOR HARMONIES AND RHYTHMIC PATTERNS allow me to share with others the essence of my creative being. Designing knitwear is like sending out personalized messages. Most times, with both the creator and the receiver, the communication is happening on a subconscious level.

My work is inspired by nature, cultures, and textiles from all over the globe. However, there are common elements of color and pattern placement woven into my work, bringing my designs together as a coherent collection.

In choosing color groups for designs, I draw exclusively from my own collection of yarn shades. Seen as one group, the 50 shades resonate with a rich pitch and tone. Within the overall group are subgroups, and within these are singular colors, each with its own unique role. Through these colors, I work intuitively, reinterpreting the world around me.

When my mother-in-law immigrated to Australia from Latvia after World War II, she brought with her a wonderful collection of craft magazines containing designs for embroidery. Many Latvians who have continued to practice their traditional crafts have retained a sophisticated understanding about the use of color and form. It is inpiring to see the intricacies of their weavings and embroidery firsthand. The Latvian sweater design in this book is created from traditional Latvian motifs.

I think my Scottish blood is always bubbling somewhere close to the surface. One of these days, I will devote an entire book to the "Pursuit for the Perfect Plaid" or to the "Attainment of an Amazing Argyle." Those subtly hand-dyed, faded kilts of old were an inspiration when I was developing my own range of woolen yarn shades.

When I create a design that is practical, visually stimulating, and timeless, I have reached the pinnacle I always strive for in my work. A few designs that I think fit this category are the "Kazak" in navy, the "Country Plaid Shirt" and the "Egyptian Bird."

I spend a lot of time experimenting with fabric ideas, knitting and reknitting swatches, trying different needle sizes, and varying the mathematics of the stitch. Working in this way, I stumbled upon the fabric for the "Cable & Moss" collection.

This fabric is elegant, soft, and flexible, unlike many cabled designs I have come across. The flexibility in the fabric was achieved by using a larger needle and by experimenting with the width of the panels. Of course, the fine Border Leicester-type fleece used in my yarn also helps to keep fabrics soft, light, and comfortable to wear.

If you've ever admired the color work in wool weaving, you'll enjoy the versatility of working with the woven stitch. I have called it "woven" because although it is a knitted stitch, it gives the appearance of being woven. I found this stitch technique in an old dictionary of knitted stitches, where it was named linen stitch. Knitted with a single color, it forms a beautiful, firm yet light and flat fabric. A blended rainbow effect is achieved when the stitch is knitted with multicolors. It's a great way to use up leftovers! You'll find this stitch in the sleeves and front bands of "Heirloom" and also in "Woven Waistcoat."

Knitted Sweater Style: Inspirations in Color expresses what my life has been about. Even as I write this, I am distracted by a parrot stealing seeds from a tree outside my studio window—its feathers are dramatic in shades of lime green, violet, and cherry red....

HOW TO USE THIS BOOK

FOR KNITTERS IN THE UNITED STATES
This book was written using measurements, needle sizes, and yarn weights that are standard in Australia. The metric system was used in all the patterns, and yarns were measured in grams. The following will help you convert these measurements:

  1 inch = 2.5 centimeters

  1 yard = 0.9 meters

  To convert centimeters to inches, divide the number of centimeters by 2.5. For example, 10 centimeters divided by 2.5 equals 4 inches.

  Most American and European yarns intended for handknitting are now labeled with their weight noted in both ounces and grams. If your yarn label does not state this dual information, know that the two most common skein/ball weights and their equivalents are:

  1¾ ounces = 50 grams

  3½ ounces = 100 grams

TENSION
The required tension is given at the start of each pattern. Before you begin knitting the garment, it is important that you knit a tension square. Using the specified needles and stitch, cast on 40 stitches and knit approximately 40 rows. Lay work flat and, without stretching, measure 10 centimeters both vertically and horizontally with a ruler. Mark with pins. Count the stitches and rows in between the pins; these should match the required tension. If not, you will need to change your needle size. Smaller needles will bring the stitches closer together, while larger needles will spread the work out. Incorrect tension will result in a misshapen garment.

YARN QUANTITIES
Quantities of yarn are based on average requirements using specified tension and Jo Sharp 8-ply DK Pure-Wool Handknitting Yarn. Responsibility cannot be accepted for the finished garment if substitute yarns are used.

SIZING
Most garments include small, medium, or large sizes, with the exception of the children's garments, which show size by age. The measurements of each garment are shown on the size diagram included with each pattern. Most of the garments are loose fitting with a drop shoulder. Note that the width of the bodice in a drop-shouldered garment adds length to the sleeve, as it falls down the shoulder and along the top of the arm. To calculate size, use a favorite sweater that fits the intended wearer well as a guide. Compare the measurements of the existing sweater with those shown on the size diagram of the garment you intend to knit, and choose the better fit.

INTARSIA
Intarsia knitting is a technique where blocks of color are worked using separate balls or bobbins of yarn,

without the yarn being carried across the back of the work between color changes. Cut lengths of yarn for each color block (an approximate gauge is to multiply the row lengths by four). Then as you knit, join in the various colors at the appropriate point on the row, and twist the yarns one over the other on the wrong side of the work to avoid holes. Darn the ends along the color join lines at the back of the work on completion of knitting.

FAIR ISLE INSTRUCTIONS

When two colors are worked repeatedly across a row, strand the yarn not in use loosely behind the stitches being worked. Spread stitches to their correct width to keep the work elastic (using a circular needle may help). If stranding more than three stitches at a time, catch the "floating" yarn at the back by weaving it under and over the color being worked.

GRAPHS

Each square on a graph represents one stitch. Unless stated, graphs are worked in stockinette stitch. When working from a graph, read odd rows (rs) from right to left and even rows (ws) from left to right. Each color used is given a number and/or a symbol. Graphs may be enlarged on a photocopier for easier reading.

CARE INSTRUCTIONS

Jo Sharp 8-ply DK Pure-Wool Handknitting Yarn is spun from premium-grade, long-fiber fleece. During processing, inferior short fibers (which can cause pilling and itching) are removed to enhance the natural softness of the yarn and to improve its wash-and-wear performance. If in the first few weeks of wear some remaining short fibers shed, these should be combed from your garment using a "de-piller" comb. With care, your Jo Sharp garment will improve with age and wear.

WASHING

For the best result, turn the garment inside out and gently hand wash in lukewarm water, using a wool detergent. Rinse thoroughly in lukewarm water. Rinse again in cold water. To remove excess moisture after washing, roll the garment inside a large towel and gently squeeze or, alternatively, spin dry the garment inside a pillow case. Dry flat in the shade. Never tumble dry.

WHY OUR YARN IS NOT MACHINE-WASH TREATED

Our yarn looks different from most other yarns—it looks natural. This is because it is not machine-wash treated, which puts a resin coating on each fiber and in effect glues fibers together, giving yarn an unnatural shiny appearance. The research we conducted before deciding not to artificially treat our yarn found that there were many knitters who preferred the natural characteristics of untreated pure-wool yarn.

PATTERN QUERIES

Write to:
Jo Sharp Pty Ltd., P.O. Box 357,
Albany, Western Australia 6330

ABBREVIATIONS

alt	alternate	kb1	knit into back of next st
approx	approximately	kfb	increase by knitting into front and back of k st
beg	beginning		
ch	chain st	m1	make one—pick up loop between sts and k into back of it
cm	centimeter		
cn	cable needle		
col(s)	color(s)	mm	millimeters
cont	continue	p	purl
c2b	cross 2 back—k into back of 2nd st on needle, then k 1st st, slipping both sts off needle at the same time	patt	pattern
		pb1	purl into back of next st
		pbf	increase by purling into back and front of p st
c2p	cross 2 purl—p into front of 2nd st on needle, then p 1st st, slipping both sts off needle together	psso	pass slipped stitch over
		rem	remain(ing)
		rep	repeat
		rev	reverse(ing)
cr2bp	slip next st onto cn, hold at back, kb1, p1 from cn	rs	right side
		sl	slip
cr2fk	slip next st onto cn, hold at front, p1, kb1 from cn	st(s)	stitch(es)
		st st	stockinette stitch
dc	double crochet	tog	together
dec	decrease	tr	treble crochet
dia	diameter	ws	wrong side
foll	follow(ing)	yb	yarn back
inc	increase	yf	yarn forward
k	knit	yon	yarn over needle
k1b	insert needle through center of st below next st on needle and knit this in the usual way, slipping the st above off the needle at the same time		

ARGYLE

WOMAN'S CARDIGAN AND CHILD'S SWEATER

This pattern is suitable for an experienced knitter with knowledge of intarsia knitting (see instructions on pp. 7-8). Both garments are drop shouldered, and the cardigan has a knitted collar.

NEEDLES
• I pair 3.25mm (USA 3) (UK 10)
• I pair 4.00mm (USA 6) (UK 8)
• Child's sweater only—3.25mm circular needle (USA 3) (UK 10) or a set of double-pointed needles

BUTTONS
Woman's cardigan—Seven 2cm

TENSION
22.5 sts and 30 rows to 10cm, measured over patterned stockinette stitch using 4.00mm needles.

YARN
Jo Sharp 8-ply DK Pure-Wool Handknitting Yarn

	Key	Color	Quantity S	(M	L)	
Woman's	1 ☐	Jade 316	12	12	13	x 50g
Cardigan	2 ☑	Violet 319	4	4	5	x 50g
	3 ⊡	Navy 327	3	3	4	x 50g
			3-5	(6-8) yo		
Child's	1 ☐	Ruby 326	5	5		x 50g
Sweater	2 ☑	Forest 318	3	4		x 50g
	3 ⊡	Navy 327	2	2		x 50g

Woman's Cardigan

BACK
Using 3.25mm needles and col 3, cast on 132 (138, 144) sts. *Work 42 rows of k2, p1 rib in the foll col sequence: 3 rows col 3, 6 rows col 2, 33 rows col 1. Change to 4.00mm needles. Using st st, beg with a k row, foll graph on p. 12 for col changes. Work 80 (88, 96) rows**.

Shape armholes Keeping patt correct, cast off 10 sts at beg of next 2 rows. Cont without further shaping for 66 rows [148 (156, 164) rows].

Shape shoulders Cast off 8 (9, 10) sts at beg of next 8 rows, and 9 (8, 7) sts at beg of foll 2 rows. Leave rem 30 sts on a st holder.

LEFT FRONT
Using 3.25mm needles and col 3, cast on 66 (69, 72) sts. Work as for back from * to **.

Shape armholes Keeping patt correct, cast off 10 sts at beg of next row. Work 50 rows.

Shape front neck Cast off 8 sts at beg of next row, patt to end. Cast off 1 st at neck edge of next and foll alt rows 7 times [41 (44, 47) sts]. Patt 3 rows [148 (156, 164) rows].

Shape shoulders Cast off 8 (9, 10) sts at beg of next and foll alt rows 4 times. Work 1 row. Cast off rem 9 (8, 7) sts.

RIGHT FRONT
Work as given for left front, rev all shaping.

SLEEVES
Using 3.25mm needles and col 3, cast on 57 sts. Work 19 rows in k2, p1 rib in foll col sequence: 3 rows col 3, 6 rows col 2, 10 rows col 1.

Next row [inc] Rib 4, [m1, rib 6] 8 times, rib 4 [65 sts]. Change to 4.00mm needles. Using st st, beg with a k row, foll graph on p. 13 for col

BACK, FRONTS & CHILD'S SLEEVE

L M S 6-8 yo 3-5 yo Child's sleeve | Right front — | — Left front Child's sleeve 3-5 yo 6-8 yo S M L

Back

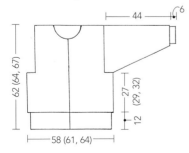

Woman's cardigan

| 44 | 6 |

62 (64, 67)

27 (29, 32)

12

58 (61, 64)

changes. AT THE SAME TIME, shape sides by inc 1 st at each end of 7th row and every foll 6th row, until there are 105 sts. Work 11 rows [132 rows] or until length desired. Cast off loosely and evenly.

MAKING UP

Press all pieces, except ribbing, gently on ws using a warm iron over a damp cloth. Using backstitch, join shoulder seams. Center sleeve into armhole and join. Join side and sleeve seams using edge-to-edge stitch on ribs.

Collar Using 4.00mm needles and col 1, cast on 6 sts. Note: The m1 abbreviation below = pick up loop between sts and k into FRONT of it.

Row 1 K2, (m1, k2 tog) twice.

Row 2 and every alt row Knit.
Rep rows 1 and 2, 3 times.

Row 9 K2, (m1, k1) twice, m1, k2.

Row 11 K2, (m1, k2 tog) twice, m1, k3.

Row 13 K2, (m1, k2 tog) twice, m1, k4.

Row 15 K2, (m1, k2 tog) twice, m1, k5.

Row 17 K2, (m1, k2 tog) twice, m1, k6.

Row 19 K2, (m1, k2 tog) twice, m1, k7.

Row 21 K2, (m1, k2 tog) twice, m1, k8.

Row 22 Cast off 6 sts, k to end of row.
Rep rows 11-22, 10 times, then rows 11-21 once. Cast off. Place collar on rs laying flat around neckhole, pin, and sew into place.

Button band Using 3.25mm needles and col 1, cast on 16 sts. K1, p1 rib until band is long enough when slightly stretched to fit along front edge of cardigan. Mark position on button band for 7 buttons, the first to come 2cm from lower edge, the last to come 1.5cm from cast-off edge, and the remainder spaced evenly between.

Buttonhole band Work as for button band, making buttonholes to correspond with button positions. Pin and sew bands into position. AT THE SAME TIME, secure and tuck collar ends into front band seams. Sew on buttons to correspond with buttonholes. Press seams.

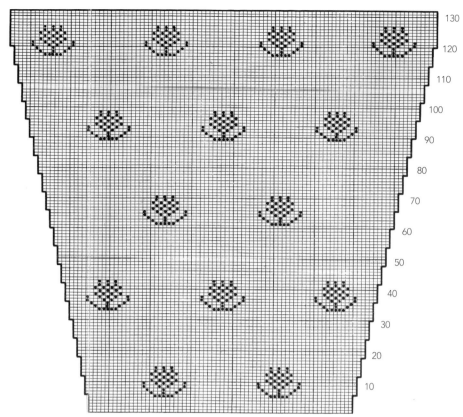

WOMAN'S SLEEVE

130
120
110
100
90
80
70
60
50
40
30
20
10

Child's Sweater

BACK

Using 3.25mm needles and col 1, cast on 98 (106) sts. Work 12 rows of k1, p1 rib. Change to 4.00mm needles. Using st st, beg with a k row, foll graph on p. 12 for col changes. Work 78 (86) rows.

Shape armholes Keeping patt correct, cast off 6 (8) sts at beg of next 2 rows.* Cont without further shaping for 44 rows [124 (132) rows].

Shape shoulders Cast off 9 (10) sts at beg of next 4 rows. Leave rem 50 sts on a st holder.

FRONT

Work as given for back to *. Cont without further shaping for 38 rows.

Shape front neck Patt 26 (30) sts, turn, and leave rem sts on a st holder. Work each side of neck separately. Cast off 2 sts at neck edge on next 5 rows [16 (20) sts].

Shape shoulders Cast off 9 (10) sts at beg of next and foll alt row. With rs facing, leave 30 sts on a st holder, rejoin yarn to rem sts, and complete second side to match first, rev all shaping.

SLEEVES

Using 3.25mm needles and col 1, cast on 34 sts. Work 11 rows in k1, p1 rib.

Next row [inc] On ws, rib 4, *m1, rib 3, rep from * to end [44 sts]. Change to 4.00mm needles. Using st st, beg with a k row, foll graph on p. 12 for col changes. AT THE SAME TIME, shape sides by inc 1 st at each end of 6 (7)th row and every foll 5 (6)th row, until there are 72 sts, taking extra sts into patt as they occur. Work 8 (11) rows [84 (102) rows] or until length desired. Cast off loosely and evenly.

MAKING UP

Press all pieces, except ribbing, gently on ws using a warm iron over a damp cloth. Using backstitch, join shoulder seams. Center sleeves into armholes and join. Join side and sleeve seams using edge-to-edge stitch on ribs.

Neckband With rs facing and using 3.25mm circular needle and col 1, pick up and k 50 sts from st holder at back of neck; 13 sts down left side front neck; 30 sts from st holder at center front; and 13 sts up right side front neck [106 sts]. Work 2.5cm in k1, p1 rib. Cast off loosely and evenly in rib. Press seams.

Child's sweater

4
28 (34)
45 (48)
26 (28.5)
4
43.5 (47)

STRAWBERRY FARM

WOMAN'S SWEATER

The Strawberry Farm sweater is drop shouldered with a rolled neckband. This pattern is suitable for a beginner knitter.

NEEDLES
- I pair 3.75mm (USA 5) (UK 9)
- I pair 4.00mm (USA 6) (UK 8)
- 3.75mm circular needle (USA 5) (UK 9) or a set of double-pointed needles

TENSION
22.5 sts and 30 rows to I0cm, measured over stockinette stitch using 4.00mm needles.

YARN
Jo Sharp 8-ply DK Pure-Wool Handknitting Yarn

Color	Quantity			
	S	(M	L)	
Satin 331	16	17	17	x 50g

BACK
Using 3.75mm needles, cast on 134 (142, 150) sts.

Row 1 On rs, k2, *p2, k2, rep from * to end.

Row 2 On rs, p2, *k2, p2, rep from * to end. Rep rows 1 and 2 until band measures 5cm, ending with a ws row. Change to 4.00mm needles. Using st st, beg with a k row, work 69 rows. Now foll graph on p. 16 for texture patt and cont for ** 121 rows [190 rows]. (Adjust length here, if desired.) Cast off.

FRONT
Work as given for back to **. Work 99 rows [168 rows]. (Adjust length here, if desired.)

Shape front neck Work 55 (59, 63) sts, turn, and leave rem sts on a st holder. Keeping patt correct, work each side of neck separately. Cast off 2 sts at neck edge on next row and foll alt rows twice, and 1 st on foll alt rows 3 times [46 (50, 54) sts]. Work 10 rows. Cast off. With rs facing, leave 24 sts on a st holder, rejoin yarn to rem sts, and complete second side to match first side, rev all shaping.

SLEEVES
Using 3.75mm needles, cast on 54 sts.

Row 1 On rs, k2, *p2, k2, rep from * to end.

Row 2 On ws, p2, *k2, p2, rep from * to end. Rep rows 1 and 2 until band measures 5cm, ending with a rs row.

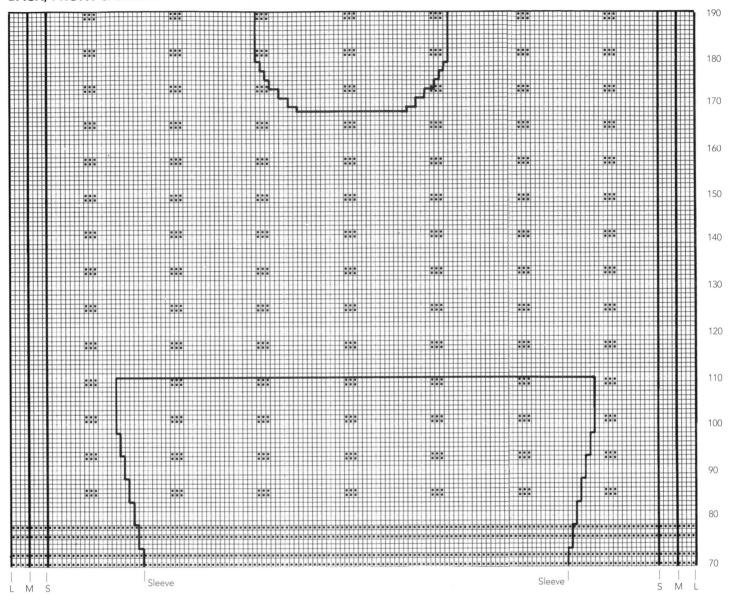

190
180
170
160
150
140
130
120
110
100
90
80
70

L M S   Sleeve   Sleeve   S M L

KEY

☐ K on rs, p on ws
▣ P on rs, k on ws

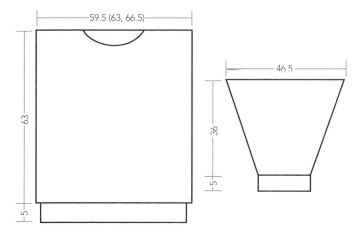

Next row (inc) Rib 2, *m1, rib 5, rep from *
9 times, m1, rib 2 [65 sts].
Change to 4.00mm needles, and cont in st st,
beg with a k row. AT THE SAME TIME, shape
sides by inc 1 st at each end of 4th row and
every foll 5th row 13 times [93 sts, 69 rows]. Now
foll graph on p. 16 for texture patt. Cont to inc
in every 5th row, as before, another 6 times
[105 sts]. Work 11 rows [110 rows]. (Adjust length
here, if desired.) Cast off loosely and evenly.

MAKING UP
Press all pieces, except ribbing, gently on ws
using a warm iron over a damp cloth. Using

backstitch, join shoulder seams. Center sleeves
and join. Join side and sleeve seams using
edge-to-edge stitch on ribs.

Neckband Using a 3.75mm circular needle, with
rs facing, pick up and k 28 sts down left side
front neck; 24 sts from st holder at center front;
28 sts up right side front neck; and 44 sts across
back neck (124 sts). Work in k2, p2 rib for 11
rounds, then k 8 rounds. Cast off. Press seams.

CACTUS FLOWER COAT

WOMAN'S CARDIGAN

This pattern is suitable for an experienced knitter with intarsia knitting skills (see instructions on pp. 7-8). The coat is drop shouldered, with the collar folded to double thickness.

NEEDLES
- 1 pair 4.00mm (USA 6) (UK 8)
- 1 pair 5.00mm (USA 8) (UK 6)

BUTTONS
Eight 2cm

TENSION
22.5 sts and 30 rows to 10cm, measured over patterned stockinette stitch using 4.00mm needles.

YARN
Jo Sharp 8-ply DK Pure-Wool Handknitting Yarn

Key		Color	Quantity			
			S	(M	L)	
1	◉	Lilac 324	11	11	11	x 50g
2		Antique 323	9	9	9	x 50g
3	◤	Gold 320	2	2	2	x 50g
4	◨	Ruby 326	2	2	2	x 50g
5	◪	Jade 316	1	1	1	x 50g
6	◡	Forest 318	1	1	1	x 50g
7	v	Violet 319	2	2	2	x 50g
8	▷	Terracotta 332	2	2	2	x 50g
9	x	Ginger 322	2	2	2	x 50g
10	•	Mulberry 325	2	2	2	x 50g
11	I	Navy 327	2	2	2	x 50g

BACK
Using 4.00mm needles and col 1, cast on 112 (118, 124) sts. Work 20 rows st st.

Rows 21 and 22 Change to 5.00mm needles and work in st st. *Forms foldline for hem.*

Row 23 Change back to 4.00mm needles and cont in st st, foll graph on pp. 20-21 for col changes. AT THE SAME TIME, shape sides by inc 1 st at each end of 65th row and every foll 14th row 5 times, then every 12th row 3 times [130 (136, 142) sts]. Cont in patt until row 262.

Shape shoulders Cast off 11 (12, 13) sts at beg of next 6 rows and 13 sts at beg of foll 2 rows. Cast off rem 38 sts.

LEFT FRONT
Using 4.00mm needles and col 1, cast on 37 (40, 43) sts. Work 20 rows st st.

Rows 21 and 22 Change to 5.00mm needles and work in st st. *Forms foldline for hem.*

Row 23 Change back to 4.00mm needles and cont in st st, foll graph on pp. 20-21 for col changes. AT THE SAME TIME, shape sides by inc 1 st at beg of 65th row and every foll 14th row 5 times, then every 12th row 3 times [46 (49, 52) sts]. Cont in patt until row 262.

Shape shoulders Cast off 11 (12, 13) sts at beg of next row and foll alt rows 2 times. Work 1 row. Cast off rem 13 sts.

RIGHT FRONT
Work as for left front, rev all shaping, and foll graph on pp. 20-21 for right front col changes.

SLEEVES
Using 4.00mm needles and col 1, cast on 77 sts. Work 20 rows st st.

Rows 21 and 22 Change to 5.00mm needles and work in st st. *Forms foldline for hem.*

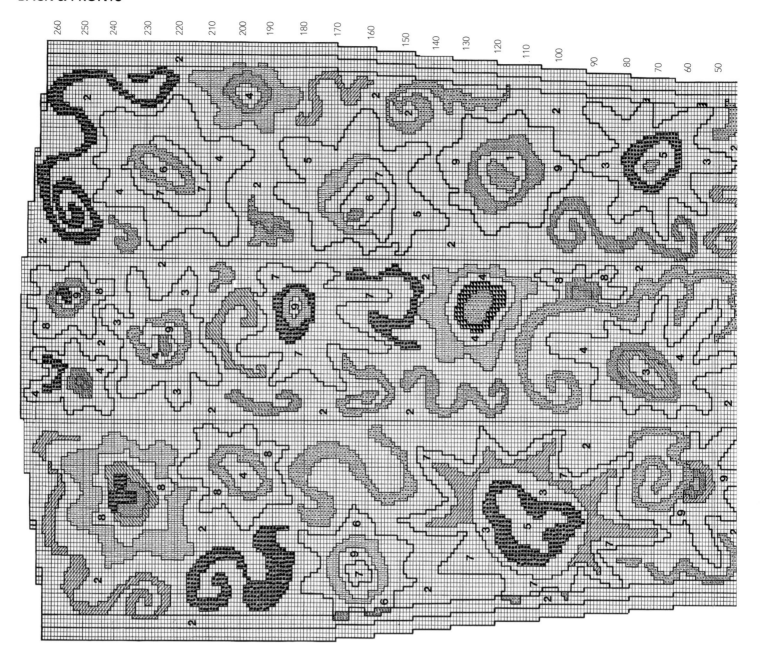

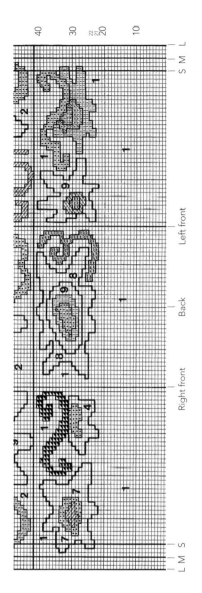

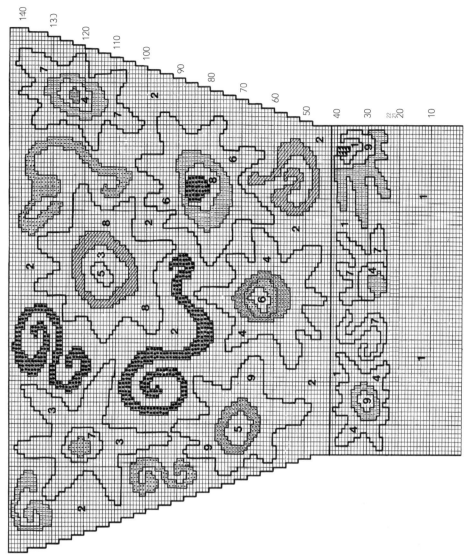

SLEEVE

Row 23 Change back to 4.00mm needles and cont in st st foll sleeve graph above right for col changes. AT THE SAME TIME, shape sides by inc 1 st at each end of 49th row and every foll 4th row 21 times, then foll 6th row once (123 sts). Work 5 rows (144 rows) or until length desired. Cast off loosely and evenly.

COLLAR
Using 4.00mm needles and col 1, cast on 60 sts. Work 4 rows st st.

Row 5 *K7, slip rem sts onto holder, turn, work these 7 sts for 5 rows, then leave on 2nd st holder. *This is the main ball of yarn; do not*

break. Attach a new length of yarn to sts on 1st holder at the buttonhole edge, k16, leave rem sts on holder, turn, and work these 16 sts for 5 rows. Break yarn and leave sts on 2nd holder. Attach new length of yarn to sts on 1st holder at buttonhole edge, k14, leave rem sts on holder, turn, and work these 14 sts for 5 rows. Break yarn and leave sts on 2nd holder. Attach new length of yarn to sts on 1st holder at buttonhole edge, k16, leave rem sts on holder, turn, and work these 16 sts for 5 rows. Break yarn and leave sts on 2nd holder. Attach new length of yarn to rem 7 sts on 1st holder, work 6 rows, leave sts on 2nd holder. Now using the main ball of yarn, knit across all sts on holder (this is row

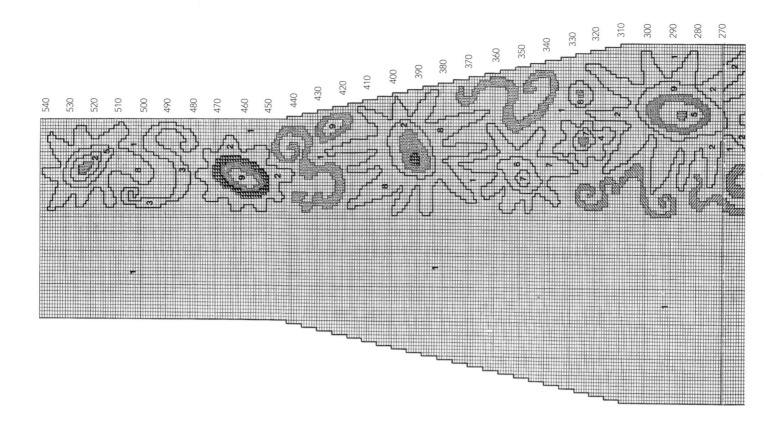

11). **Cont on in st st for 21 rows. Rep from * twice, then from * to ** once (95 rows). Cont foll collar graph above for col changes.

AT THE SAME TIME, shape sides by inc 1 st at each end of 99th row and every foll 6th row 22 times (106 sts). Work 79 rows, then dec 1 st at each end of next row and foll 6th row 22 times (60 sts). Cont these 60 sts for 97 rows. Cast off.

MAKING UP

Press all pieces gently on ws using a warm iron over a damp cloth. Using backstitch, join shoulder seams. Center sleeves and join. Join side and sleeve seams.

Fold collar in half lengthwise, rs facing, and join bottom edges together. Now turn to ws facing and pin the two edges to jacket body, starting from center back, down to foldline of front hems, stretching slightly. Sew into place.

For each buttonhole at front, find a partner on underside, then buttonhole stitch the two together using col 1. Sew buttons onto collar to correspond with buttonholes. Turn bodice and sleeve hems along foldlines and sl st into place. Press seams.

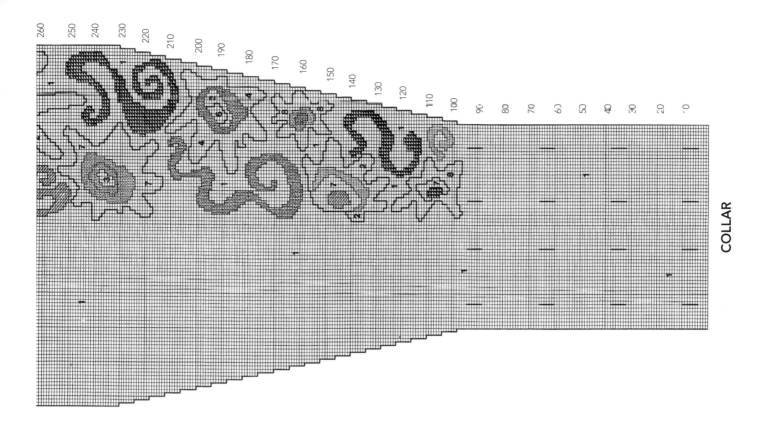

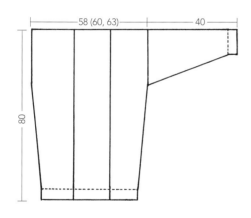

58 (60, 63) — 40

80

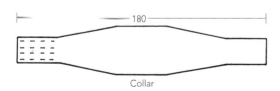

180

Collar

LATVIAN

WOMAN'S AND MAN'S SWEATER

This garment is suitable for an experienced knitter with knowledge of Fair Isle knitting. It is a loose-fitting, drop-shouldered sweater.

NEEDLES
- 1 pair 3.25mm (USA 3) (UK 10)
- 1 pair 4.00mm or 4.00mm circular needle 80cm (USA 6) (UK 8)
- 3.25mm circular needle 40cm (USA 3) (UK 10) or a set of 4 double-pointed needles

TENSION
25 sts and 26 rows to 10cm, measured over Fair Isled stockinette stitch using 4.00mm needles.

YARN
Jo Sharp 8-ply DK Pure-Wool Handknitting Yarn

Key	Color	Quantity S	(M	L)	
A ☐	Antique 323	10	11	12	x 50g
B ⊡	Black 302	10	11	12	x 50g

BACK
Using 4.00mm needles and col A, cast on 152 (160, 168) sts. Then, joining in col B, cont in k2, p2 rib as follows:

Row 1 On rs, (k2 col B, p2 col A) to end.

Row 2 On ws, (k2 col A, p2 col B) to end. Repeat these 2 rows 9 times (20 rows). Now using st st and beg with a k row, foll graph on p. 26 for color changes. *Work 156 (160, 164) rows.

Shape shoulders Cast off 10 (11, 12) sts at the beg of next 8 rows, then 13 (13, 13) sts at beg of next 2 rows. Leave rem 46 sts on a holder.

FRONT
Work as given for back to *. Work 132 (136, 140) rows.

Shape front neck Patt 63 (67, 71) sts, turn, and leave rem sts on a holder. Work each side of neck separately. Cast off 1 st at neck edge on next and foll rows 6 times [57 (61, 65) sts] and 1 st on foll alt rows 4 times [53 (57, 61) sts]. Patt 9 rows without further shaping.

Shape shoulders Cast off 10 (11, 12) sts at beg of next and foll alt rows 4 times. Work 1 row, then cast off rem 13 (13, 13) sts. With rs facing, leave 26 sts on holder, rejoin yarn to rem sts, and complete second side to match first side, rev all shaping.

SLEEVES
Using 3.25mm needles and col A, cast on 60 sts. Join in col B and work 19 rows in two-col rib, as given for back, ending with a rs row.

FRONT, BACK & SLEEVE

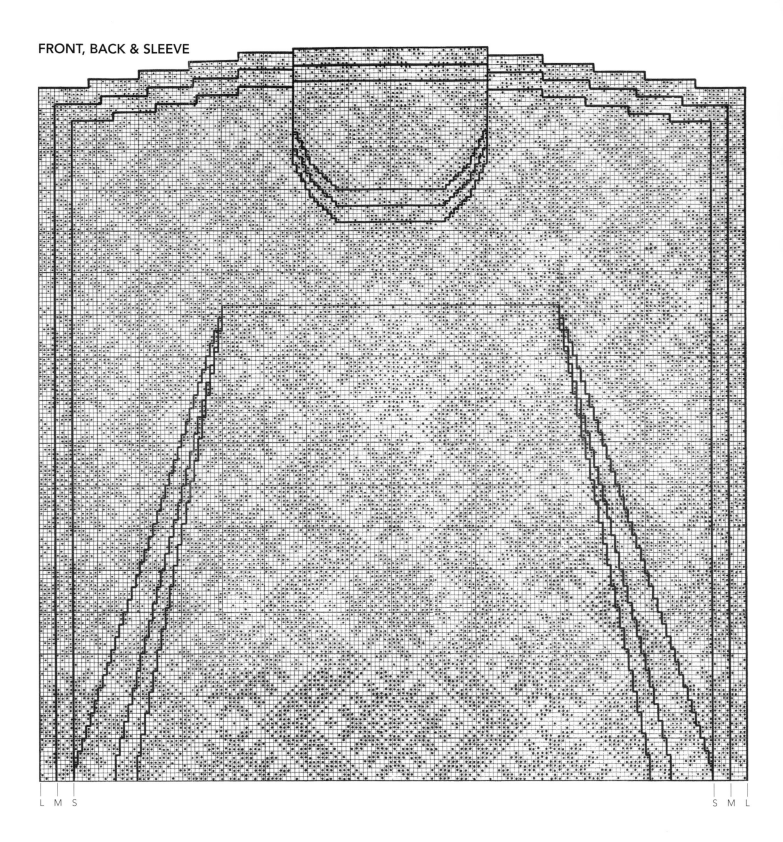

L M S   S M L

Next row (inc) Rib 1 (m1, rib 3) 19 times, m1, rib 2 (80 sts). Change to 4.00mm needles. Using st st and beg with a k row, foll graph on p. 26 for col changes. AT THE SAME TIME, shape sides by inc 1 st at each end of 7th (7th, 4th) row and every foll 5th (4th, 3rd) row until there are 122 (132, 152) sts. Take extra sts into patt as they occur. Work 5 (5, 3) rows (112 rows). Cast off loosely and evenly.

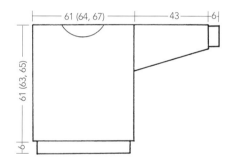

MAKING UP

Press all pieces, except ribbing, gently on ws using a warm iron over a damp cloth. Using backstitch, join shoulder seams. Center sleeves and join. Join side and sleeve seams using edge-to-edge stitch on ribs.

Neckband Using a 3.25mm circular needle and cols A and B, with rs facing, pick up and k2 col A, k2 col B, 44 sts down left side front neck; 26 sts from st holder across front neck; 44 sts up right side front neck; and 46 sts from st holder across back of neck (160 sts). Work 4.5cm in k2, p2 two-col rib (as given for back), working in rounds. Using col A, cast off evenly in rib. Press seams.

NARRIKUP

MAN'S SWEATER

This classic, loose-fitting, drop-shouldered sweater features an easily knitted texture pattern. The sweater is suitable for a beginner knitter.

NEEDLES
- 1 pair 3.75mm (USA 5) (UK 9)
- 1 pair 4.00mm (USA 6) (UK 8)
- 3.75mm circular needle (USA 5) (UK 9) or a set of double-pointed needles

TENSION
22.5 sts and 34 rows to 10cm, measured over texture pattern using 4.00mm needles.

TEXTURE PATTERN
Row 1 On rs, knit.
Row 2 On ws, purl.
Row 3 K1, p2 to end.
Row 4 Purl.
Repeat these 4 rows.

YARN
Jo Sharp 8-ply DK Pure-Wool Handknitting Yarn

Color	Quantity		
	S	(M	L)
Smoke 339	17	18	18

BACK
Using 3.75mm needles, cast on 134 (142, 150) sts. Work in k2, p2 rib for 20 rows. Change to 4.00mm needles, and work in texture patt for* 214 rows (adjust length here, if desired). Cast off.

FRONT
Work as given for back to *. Work 190 rows (adjust length here, if desired).

Shape front neck Keeping texture patt correct, work 55 (59, 63) sts, turn, and leave rem sts on a st holder. Work each side of neck separately. Cast off 2 sts at neck edge on next row and foll alt rows twice, and 1 st on foll alt rows 3 times [46 (50, 54) sts]. Work 12 rows. Cast off.
With rs facing, leave 24 sts on a st holder, rejoin yarn to rem sts, and complete second side to match first side, rev all shaping.

SLEEVES
Using 3.75mm needles, cast on 62 sts. Work in k2, p2 rib for 19 rows, ending with a rs row.

Next row (inc) Rib 6, *m1, rib 5, rep from * 9 times, m1, rib 6 (73 sts). Change to 4.00mm needles, and work in texture patt. AT THE SAME TIME, shape sides by inc 1 st at each end of 7th row and every foll 6th row 19 times (113 sts). Work 25 rows (146 rows). (Adjust length here, if desired.) Cast off loosely and evenly.

MAKING UP
Press all pieces, except ribbing, gently on ws using a warm iron over a damp cloth. Using backstitch, join shoulder seams. Center sleeves and join. Join side and sleeve seams using edge-to-edge stitch on ribs.

Neckband
Using a 3.75mm circular needle, with rs facing, pick up and k 28 sts down left side front neck; 24 sts from st holder at center front; 28 sts up right side front neck; and 44 sts across back neck (124 sts). Work in k2, p2 rib for 11 rounds. Knit 8 rounds. Cast off. Press seams.

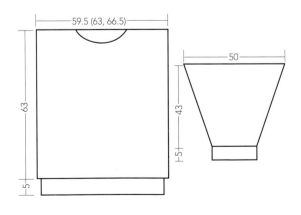

CHINESE TAPESTRY

WOMAN'S VEST

The Chinese Tapestry vest has a knitted lace border and crochet edging. This pattern is easy to follow and is suitable for an average knitter with knowledge of intarsia knitting (see instructions on pp. 7-8).

NEEDLES
- I pair 4.00mm (USA 6) (UK 8)
- 3.50mm crochet hook (USA E/4) (UK 9)

BUTTONS
Four 1.5cm

TENSION
22.5 sts and 30 rows to 10cm, measured over patterned stockinette stitch using 4.00mm needles.

YARN
Jo Sharp 8-ply DK Pure-Wool Handknitting Yarn

Key		Color	Quantity		
			M	**(L)**	
1	☐	Earth 334	9	9	x 50g
2	⊡	Violet 319	1	1	x 50g
3	◹	Lilac 324	1	1	x 50g
4	⩗	Jade 316	1	1	x 50g
5	⊡	Forest 318	1	1	x 50g
6	⊞	Ruby 326	1	1	x 50g
7	⊡	Brick 333	1	1	x 50g
8	◪	Terracotta 332	1	1	x 50g
9	⊠	Wedgewood 340	1	1	x 50g
10	■	Antique 323	1	1	x 50g
11	⊏	Chartreuse 330	1	1	x 50g
12	◿	Wine 307	1	1	x 50g
13	⊟	Linen 335	1	1	x 50g

BACK
Using 4.00mm needles and col 1, cast on 118 (124) sts. Using st st, beg with a k row, foll graph on p. 32 for col changes. Work 90 (94) rows.

Shape armholes Cast off 6 (7) sts at beg of next 2 rows, and 2 (2) sts at beg of foll 6 rows [94 (98) sts]. Cont without further shaping for 70 (70) rows.

Shape shoulders and back neck
Cast off 5 (7) sts at beg of next 2 rows. Cast off 7 (7) sts at beg of next row, patt 18 sts, turn, and leave rem sts on a holder. Work each side of neck separately. Cast off 2 sts at beg of next row (ws) and foll alt row twice. AT THE SAME TIME, cast off 7 sts at beg of foll rs rows twice. With rs facing, rejoin yarn to rem sts. Cast off center 34 sts. Complete second side to match first side, rev all shaping.

LEFT FRONT
Using 4.00mm needles and col 1, cast on 65 (68) sts. Using st st, beg with a k row, foll graph on p. 32 for col changes. Work 66 (70) rows.

Shape neck Dec 1 st at end (neck edge) of next and foll 4th row 6 times [59 (62) sts]. Work 3 rows.

Shape armholes Cast off 6 (7) sts at beg (armhole edge) of next row and 2 sts at beg of foll alt rows 3 times. AT THE SAME TIME, dec 1 st at end (neck edge) of next row and foll 4th rows, as before, another 20 times. Work 1 row [27 (29) sts].

Shape shoulders Cast off 5 (7) sts at beg of next row and 7 (7) sts at beg of foll alt rows 3 times. Dec once more at neck edge, as before.

RIGHT FRONT
Work as given for left front, rev all shaping.

BACK & FRONTS

L M   Left front   Right front   M L

MAKING UP

Press all pieces gently on ws using a warm iron over a damp cloth. Using backstitch, join shoulder seams and side seams.

Lace border Using 4.00mm needles and col 1, cast on 14 sts.

Row 1 On ws, k2, yf, k2 tog, k5, yf, k2 tog, yf, k3.

Row 2 and every alt row K1, yf, k2 tog, k to end.

Row 3 K2, yf, k2 tog, k4, [yf, k2 tog] twice, yf, k3.

Row 5 K2, yf, k2 tog, k3, [yf, k2 tog] 3 times, yf, k3.

Row 7 K2, yf, k2 tog, k2, [yf, k2 tog] 4 times, yf, k3.

Row 9 K2, yf, k2 tog, k1, [yf, k2 tog] 5 times, yf, k3.

Row 11 K2, yf, k2 tog, k1, k2 tog, [yf, k2 tog] 5 times, k2.

Row 13 K2, yf, k2 tog, k2, k2 tog, [yf, k2 tog] 4 times, k2.

Row 15 K2, yf, k2 tog, k3, k2 tog, [yf, k2 tog] 3 times, k2.

Row 17 K2, yf, k2 tog, k4, k2 tog, [yf, k2 tog] twice, k2.

Row 19 K2, yf, k2 tog, k5, k2 tog, yf, k2 tog, k2.

Row 20 K1, yf, k2 tog, k to end.
Rep these 20 rows until border is long enough to fit around bottom of vest, ending with a 20th row. Cast off.
With rs facing, pin border to bottom of vest and sl st into position.

Crochet neck edging Using a 3.50mm crochet hook and col 1, join yarn with a sl st to bottom edge of lace border on right front. Work 3 ch, 3 tr in same spot, *miss approx 1cm, 1 dc, miss approx 1cm, 4 tr in same spot, rep from * up right front edge, around back of neck and down left front edge, spacing sts so that edging lies flat and there are the same number of treble clusters on both sides.

Buttons Sew buttons to center of treble clusters on left front. Place first button at start of neck shaping and last button where lace border joins body, with the remaining two spaced evenly between. Each button fastens through the center of a treble cluster on right front.

Crochet armhole edging Work as given for neck edging. Press seams.

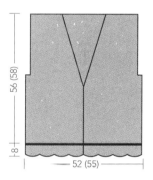

56 (58)

8

52 (55)

COUNTRY PLAID SHIRT

WOMAN'S CARDIGAN

The Country Plaid Shirt is suitable for an average knitter with knowledge of intarsia knitting (see instructions on pp. 7-8). This sweater features a crew neck and moss stitch-bordered splits at the sides.

NEEDLES
- I pair 3.75mm (USA 5) (UK 9)
- I pair 4.00mm (USA 6) (UK 8)

BUTTONS
Six 2cm

TENSION
22.5 sts and 30 rows to 10cm, measured over patterned stockinette stitch using 4.00mm needles.

YARN
Jo Sharp 8-ply DK Pure-Wool Handknitting Yarn

Key	Color	Quantity S	(M	L)	
1	Slate 328	7	8	9	x 50g
2	Khaki 329	4	4	5	x 50g
3	Ginger 322	2	2	3	x 50g
4	Earth 334	2	2	2	x 50g
5	Linen 335	1	1	1	x 50g
6	Wine 307	2	2	2	x 50g
7	Smoke 339	2	2	2	x 50g
8	Antique 323	1	1	1	x 50g
9	Gold 320	1	1	1	x 50g

BACK
Using 4.00mm needles and col 2, cast on 141 (149, 157) sts.

Beg moss st patt, row 1 K1, *p1, k1, rep from * to end. Rep row 1 for moss st patt. Work another 3 rows moss st patt, then change to col 1 and work 8 rows more, inc 1 st in center of last row [142 (150, 158) sts].

Beg graph patt Rep rows 1 through 52, foll graph on pp. 36-37 for patt. Cont working first and last 5 sts in moss st patt using col 1 and rem sts in st st patt from graph for 30 rows, then all sts in st st patt until 204 (208, 212) rows in total have been worked.

Next row Cast off first 51 (54, 57) sts loosely, patt 40 (42, 44), cast off last 51 (54, 57) sts loosely. Leave rem 40 (42, 44) sts on a st holder.

LEFT FRONT
Using 4.00mm needles and col 2, cast on 71 (75, 79) sts. Work 4 rows in moss st patt as given for back, then change to col 1 and work 8 rows more.**

Beg graph patt Rep rows 1 through 52, foll graph on pp. 36-37 for patt. Cont working first 5 sts in moss st patt using col 1 and rem sts in st st patt from graph for 30 rows, then all sts in st st patt until 183 (185, 187) rows in total have been worked.

Next row, shape front neck On ws, p and slip next 11 (12, 13) sts onto a st holder, patt to end. Cont in patt on these 60 (63, 66) sts and cast off 2 sts at neck edge in alt rows 3 times, then dec 1 st at neck edge in next and alt rows, 3 times in all [51 (54, 57) sts]. Work 9 (11, 13) rows. Cast off.

BACK & FRONTS

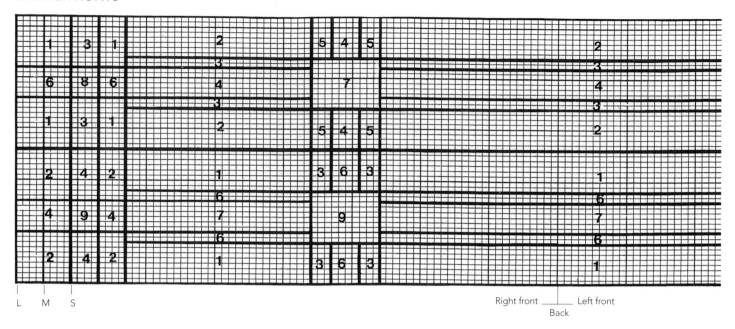

L M S

Right front ⌐ Left front
Back

RIGHT FRONT
Work as for left front to **.

Beg graph patt Rep rows 1 through 52, foll graph above for patt. Cont working last 5 sts in moss st patt using col 1 and rem sts in st st patt from graph for 30 rows, then all sts in st st patt until 182 (184, 186) rows in total have been worked.

Next row, shape front neck On rs, k and slip next 11 (12, 13) sts onto a st holder, patt to end. Cont in patt on these 60 (63, 66) sts and cast off 2 sts at neck edge in alt rows 3 times, then dec 1 st at neck edge in alt rows, 3 times in all [51 (54, 57) sts]. Work 9 (11, 13) rows. Cast off.

SLEEVES
Using 3.75mm needles and col 1, cast on 51 (55, 59) sts. Work 12 rows moss st patt as given for back, inc 1 st in center of last row [52 (56, 60) sts].
Change to 4.00mm needles. Using st st, beg with a k row and work 68 rows. AT THE SAME TIME, shape sides by inc 1 st at each end of 3rd row and every foll 4th row 16 times [86 (90, 94) sts]. Cont in st st and work 38 rows patt foll graph on p. 37 for col changes. AT THE SAME TIME, shape sides by inc 1 st at each end of 3rd row and every foll 4th row 7 times [102 (106, 110) sts]. Cast off loosely and evenly.

MAKING UP
Press all pieces, except moss st bands, gently on ws using a warm iron over a damp cloth. Using backstitch, join shoulder seams. Center sleeves and join. Join side and sleeve seams, leaving sides of back and fronts open along moss st edges.

Button band Using 3.75mm needles and col 1, cast on 9 sts. Work 242 rows moss st patt as given for back. Leave sts on a spare needle. Break off yarn.

Buttonhole band Using 3.75mm needles and col 1, cast on 9 sts. Work 6 rows moss st patt.

Row 7 Patt 3, cast off next 3 sts, patt 3.

Row 8 Patt 3, cast on 3 sts, patt 3 (buttonhole). Work 46 rows in moss st patt. Rep last 48 rows 3 times, then rows 7 and 8 once (5 buttonholes). Work 43 rows moss st patt. Leave sts on needle. Do not break off yarn.

Neckband With rs facing, using 3.75mm needle to hold buttonhole band sts and col 1, k across 11 (12, 13) sts on right front st holder, pick up and k 19 (21, 23) sts evenly along right front neck edge. K across 40 (42, 44) sts from back st holder, pick up and k 20 (22, 24) sts evenly along left front neck edge. K across 11 (12, 13) sts on

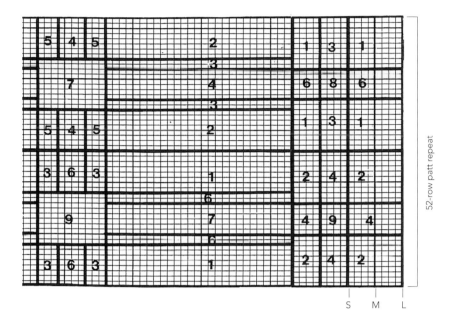

52-row patt repeat

S M L

left front st holder, then patt across button band sts [119 (127, 135) sts]. Work 3 rows moss st patt.

Next row Patt 3, cast off next 3 sts, patt to end.

Next row Patt to last 3 sts, cast on 3 sts, patt 3 (6 buttonholes in all). Work 6 rows moss st patt. Cast off loosely in patt. Sew rem front bands into place. Sew on buttons to correspond with buttonholes.

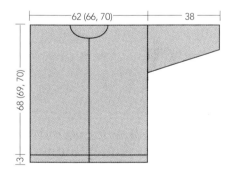

62 (66, 70)   38

68 (69, 70)

3

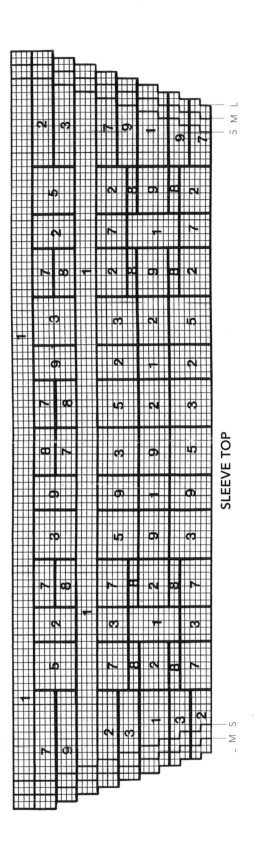

SLEEVE TOP

S M L

M S

EGYPTIAN BIRD

WOMAN'S SWEATER

The Egyptian Bird sweater is suitable for an experienced knitter with knowledge of intarsia knitting (see instructions on pp. 7-8).

NEEDLES
• 1 pair 3.75mm (USA 5) (UK 9)
• 1 pair 4.00mm (USA 6) (UK 8)
• 3.75mm circular needle (USA 5) (UK 9) or a set of double-pointed needles
• Embroidery needle

TENSION
22.5 sts and 30 rows to 10 cm, measured over patterned stockinette stitch using 4.00mm needles.

YARN
Jo Sharp 8-ply DK Pure-Wool Handknitting Yarn

Key		Color	Quantity			
			S	(M	L)	
1	◪	Brick 333	12	13	13	x 50g
2	·	Ginger 322	3	3	3	x 50g
3	▨	Jade 316	1	1	1	x 50g
4	□	Olive 313	1	1	1	x 50g
5	⊡	Violet 319	1	1	1	x 50g
6	⊡	Gold 320	1	1	1	x 50g
7	◩	Renaissance 312	1	1	1	x 50g
8	⊞	Naples 321	1	1	1	x 50g

BACK
Using 3.75mm needles and col 2, cast on 132 (138,144) sts. Work in moss st rib as follows:

Row 1 On rs, *k3, p1, k1, p1, rep from * to end.

Row 2 P1, *k1, p5, rep from * to last 5 sts, k1, p4. Change to col 1 and rep rows 1 and 2 until band measures 5cm and ends with a ws row. Change to 4.00mm needles. Using st st, beg with k row, foll graph on p. 40 for col changes. **Work 182 (190, 198) rows. Cast off 44 (47, 50) sts at beg of next two rows. Leave rem 44 sts on a holder.

FRONT
Work as given for back to **. Work 148 (156,164) rows.

Shape front neck Patt 54 (57, 60) sts, turn, and leave rem sts on a holder. Work each side of neck separately. Cast off 1 st at neck edge on next 6 rows and 1 st on foll alt rows 4 times [44 (47, 50) sts]. Patt 19 rows. Cast off. With rs facing, leave 24 sts on a holder. Rejoin yarn to rem sts and complete second side to match first side, rev all shaping.

SLEEVES
Using 3.75mm needles and col 2, cast on 54 sts. Work 2 rows in moss st rib. Change to col 1 and cont in moss st rib until work measures 4cm and ends with a rs row.

Next row (inc) Rib 2, [m1, rib 5] 10 times, m1, rib 2 [65 sts].
Change to 4.00mm needles, and using st st, beg with a k row, foll graph on p. 41 for col changes. AT THE SAME TIME, shape sides by inc 1 st at each end of 7th row and every foll 6th row 10 times, and every foll 4th row 9 times [105 sts]. Work 5 rows [108 rows] or until length desired. Cast off loosely and evenly.

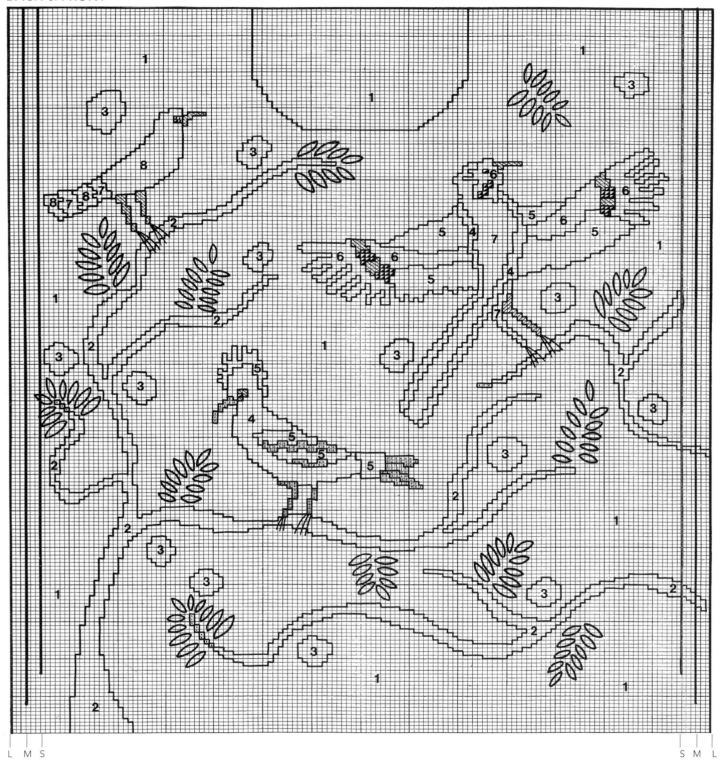

MAKING UP

Press all pieces, except ribbing, gently on ws using a warm iron over a damp cloth. Using backstitch, join shoulder seams. Center sleeves and join.

Embroidery

Using col 2, embroider leaves with lazy daisy stitch, as shown on graphs above and on p. 41. Embroider bird's feet using same col as legs with split piece of yarn and stem stitch. Join side and sleeve seams using edge-to-edge stitch on ribs.

SLEEVE

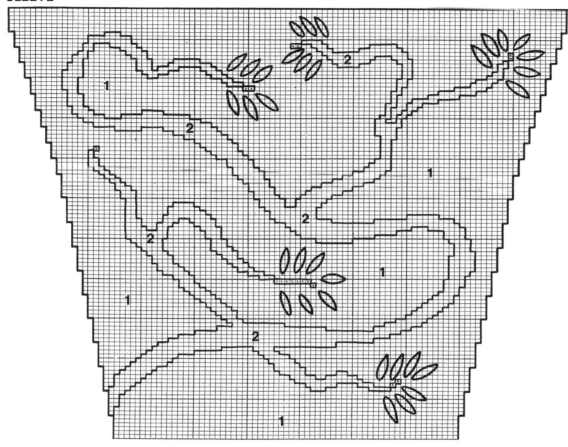

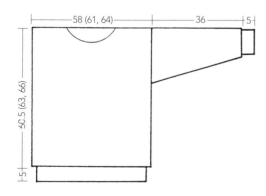

Neckband

Using a 3.75mm circular needle and col 1, with rs facing, pick up and k 38 sts down left side of front neck; 24 st from holder at center front; 38 sts up right side of front neck; and 44 sts from st holder at back neck [144 sts]. Work 14 rounds in moss st rib. Change to col 2, work 2 rounds in rib as set. Cast off evenly. Press seams.

FISHERMAN'S GANSEY

WOMAN'S AND MAN'S SWEATER

The Fisherman's Gansey is a loose-fitting, drop-shouldered sweater with a wrapped collar. This pattern is easy to follow and is suitable for a beginner knitter.

NEEDLES
- I pair 3.25mm (USA 3) (UK 10)
- I pair 3.75mm (USA 5) (UK 9)
- I pair 4.00mm (USA 6) (UK 8)

TENSION
22.5 sts and 30 rows to 10cm, measured over stockinette stitch using 4.00mm needles.

SIZING NOTE
This pattern shows two necklines and two sleeve shapes (man's and woman's). The collar is in one size and fits both necklines. For the front and back, there are three sizes shown, suitable for both man and woman.

YARN
Jo Sharp 8-ply DK Pure-Wool Handknitting Yarn

	Color	Quantity			
		S	(M	L)	
Woman's Sweater	Forest 318	16	17	17	x 50g
Man's Sweater	Mulberry 325	18	18	19	x 50g

BACK
Using 3.25mm needles, cast on 134 (140, 146) sts. Work 30 rows, referring to Graph 1 on p. 44 for texture patt.

Row 31 Change to 4.00mm needles, and cont in st st for 86 (92, 98) rows [116 (122, 128) rows]. Adjust length here if required. Now refer to Graph 2 on p. 44 for texture patt and * foll until 216 (222, 228) rows are completed.

Shape shoulders Cont to foll graph for texture patt, cast off 8 (9, 10) sts at beg of next 6 rows and 10 (10, 10) sts at beg of foll 4 rows. Cast off rem 46 sts.

FRONT
(Woman's neckline shown in italics.) Work as for back until *. Foll until 202 (208, 214) rows are completed.

Shape front neck Patt 59 *(62, 65)*, 53 *(56, 59)* sts, turn, and leave rem sts on a holder. Work each side of neck separately. Cast off 2 sts at beg of next and foll alt rows 3 times, then 1 st at beg of foll alt rows 3 times *[50 (53, 56)*, 44 *(47, 50)* sts]. Patt 2 rows.

Shape shoulders Cast off 8 (9, 10) sts at beg of next and foll alt rows 3 times, and 10 (10, 10) sts at beg of foll alt rows twice. *Work 1 row and cast off rem 6 (6, 6) sts.* With rs facing, rejoin yarn to rem sts, cast off center 16 *(28)* sts and patt to end. Complete second side to match first side, rev all shaping.

SLEEVES
(Woman's size shown in italics.) Using 3.25mm needles, cast on *54* (62) sts. Work 30 rows referring to Graph 1 on p. 44 for texture patt.

GRAPH 1

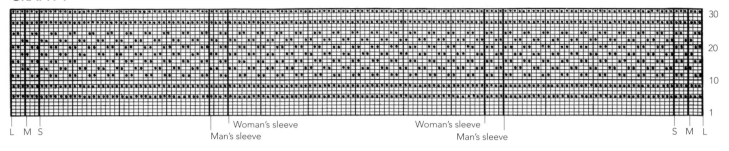

L M S
Woman's sleeve
Man's sleeve
Woman's sleeve
Man's sleeve
S M L

30
20
10
1

GRAPH 2

Man's neckline   Woman's neckline   Man's neckline

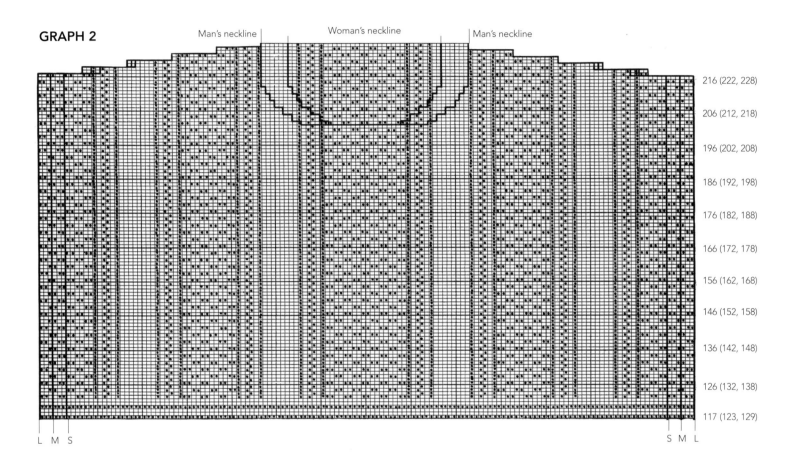

L M S

S M L

216 (222, 228)
206 (212, 218)
196 (202, 208)
186 (192, 198)
176 (182, 188)
166 (172, 178)
156 (162, 168)
146 (152, 158)
136 (142, 148)
126 (132, 138)
117 (123, 129)

GRAPH 3

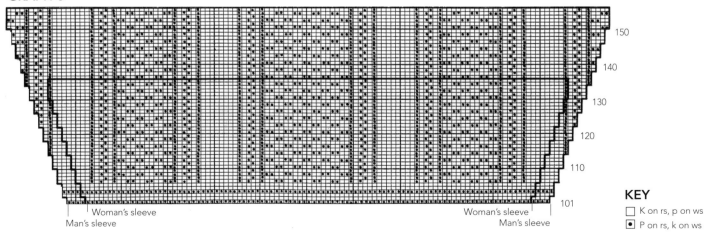

Woman's sleeve
Man's sleeve
Woman's sleeve
Man's sleeve

150
140
130
120
110
101

KEY

☐ K on rs, p on ws

▣ P on rs, k on ws

Row 31 Change to 4.00mm needles, and cont in st st for *70* (70) rows. AT THE SAME TIME, inc 1 st at each end of this row and foll alt rows *6* (6) times, then every 4th row *14* (14) times [*96* (104) sts]. Now refer to Graph 3 on p. 44 for texture patt, inc as before until there are *112* (130) sts. Patt *5* (5) rows [*136* (156) rows]. Cast off loosely and evenly.

COLLAR
Using 3.75mm needles, cast on 42 sts. Working in k2, p2 rib, inc 2 sts at each end of every row until there are 162 sts. Cast off loosely and evenly.

MAKING UP
Press all pieces gently on ws using a warm iron over a damp cloth. Using backstitch, join shoulder seams. Center sleeves and join. Join side and sleeve seams. Fold bottom edge and sleeve edge along first garter st row to inside and sl st this hem into place. On rs, pin shaped edge of collar to neckhole, overlapping at front. Sew into position. Press seams and hems.

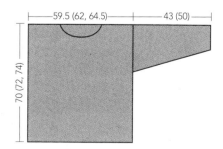

EMBROIDERED ROSE

WOMAN'S CARDIGAN

The Embroidered Rose cardigan is suitable for an average knitter with basic needlework skills. The sweater is loose fitting and drop shouldered with a moss stitch rib.

NEEDLES
- 1 pair 3.75mm (USA 5) (UK 9)
- 1 pair 4.00mm (USA 6) (UK 8)
- Embroidery needle

BUTTONS
Five 1.7cm

TENSION
22.5 sts and 30 rows to 10 cm, measured over patterned stockinette stitch using 4.00mm needles.

YARN
Jo Sharp 8-ply DK Pure-Wool Handknitting Yarn

Key	Color	Quantity			
		S	(M	L)	
1	Renaissance 312	14	15	15	x 50g
2	Brick 333	1	1	1	x 50g
	Jade 316	1	1	1	x 50g
	Gold 320	1	1	1	x 50g
	Ginger 322	1	1	1	x 50g
	Daisy 315	1	1	1	x 50g

BACK
Using 3.75mm needles and col 2, cast on 132 (138, 144) sts. Work in moss st rib as follows:

Row 1 On rs, * k3, p1, k1, p1 rep from * to end.

Row 2 P1, * k1, p5, rep from * to last 5 sts, k1, p4. Change to col 1 and rep rows 1 and 2 until band measures 5cm and ends with a ws row. Change to 4.00mm needles. Using st st, beg with k row, ** work 156 (164, 172) rows. Cast off.

LEFT FRONT
Using 3.75mm needles and col 2, cast on 66 (66, 72) sts. Work as given for back to **. Work 84 (92, 100) rows.

Shape front neck Dec 1 st at neck edge on next and foll 4th rows, 18 times. Work 3 rows. Cast off.

RIGHT FRONT
Work as given for left front, rev all shaping.

SLEEVES
Using 3.75mm needles and col 2, cast on 54 sts. Work 2 rows in moss st rib. Change to col 1 and cont in moss st rib until work measures 4cm and ends with a rs row.

Next row (inc) Rib 2, [m1, rib 5] 10 times, m1, rib 2 [65 sts]. Change to 4.00mm needles and beg with a k row, cont in st st. AT THE SAME TIME, shape sides by inc 1 st at each end of 7th row and every foll 6th row 10 times, and every foll 4th row 9 times [105 sts]. Work 5 rows [108 rows] or until length desired. Cast off loosely and evenly.
See the illustration on p. 48 for large blossom design. Each blossom uses Daisy 315 for the spikes around the central lazy daisy blossom. Use Ginger 322 for the outermost circle on all blossoms. The central lazy daisy blossom and

EMBROIDERY

Key	Color	
←←←	Brick 333	Split thread, stem stitch stems and lazy daisy stitch leaves.
--←--←--	Jade 316	Same instructions as for Brick 333.
✳	Gold 320	Use full thread, lazy daisy stitch small blossoms. Use Daisy 315 and a French knot for center.
✖	Ginger 322	Same instructions as for Gold 320.

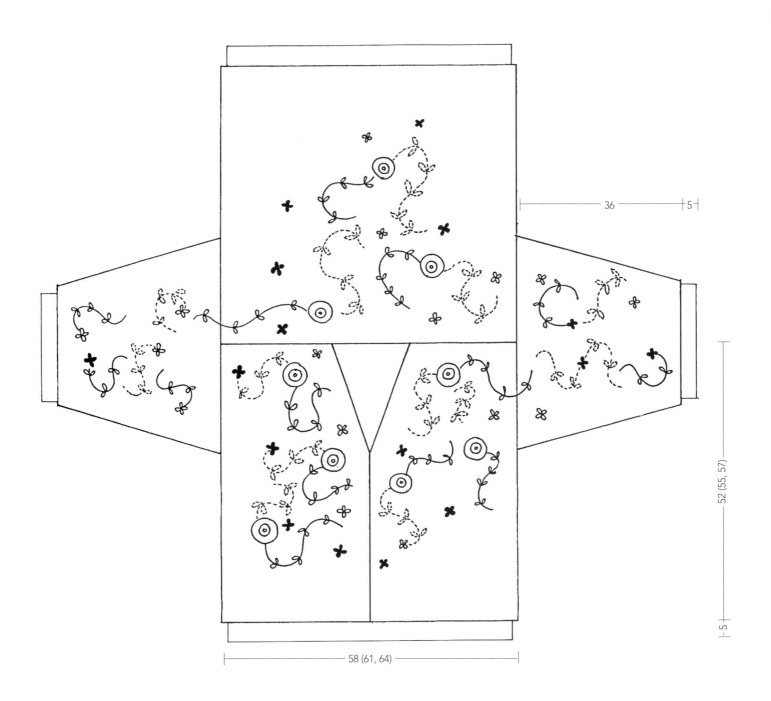

36 ⊢5⊣

52 (55, 57)

⊢5⊣

58 (61, 64)

two inner circles are embroidered using Jade 316, Brick 333, and Gold 320. Alternate the order of these three shades.

To split thread: Yarn is made up of four strands of wool. Divide these into two groups of two and pull apart.

MAKING UP

Press all pieces, except ribbing, gently on ws using a warm iron over a damp cloth. Using backstitch, join shoulder seams. Center sleeves and join. Join side and sleeve seams using edge-to-edge stitch on ribs.

Button band With ws facing, using 3.75mm needles and col 1, pick up and k 78 (84, 90) sts evenly along left front from bottom edge to beg of neck shaping. Work 6 rows in moss st rib. Change to col 2 and work a further 2 rows in moss st rib as set. Cast off evenly in rib. Mark position on button band for 5 buttons, the first to come 2cm up from lower edge, the last to come 1cm down from top edge, and the remainder spaced evenly between. Sew on buttons.

Buttonhole band Work as for button band, making buttonholes to correspond with position of buttons.

Collar Using 4.00mm needles and col 2, cast on 183 sts.

Row 1 * K3, p1, k1, p1, rep from * to last 3 sts, k3.

Row 2 P4, * k1, p5, rep from * to last 5 sts, k1, p4. Change to col 1 and rep rows 1 and 2, 3 times. Cast off 3 sts at beg of next 14 rows, then 4 sts at beg of next 22 rows, keeping rib patt correct [53 sts]. Cast off evenly in rib as set. Using edge-to-edge stitch, attach cast-off edge of collar piece to neckhole. Press seams.

GALAXY

WOMAN'S, MAN'S, AND CHILD'S SWEATER

The Galaxy sweater is drop shouldered and loose fitting. This pattern is easy to follow and is suitable for an average knitter with knowledge of intarsia knitting (see instructions on pp. 7-8).

NEEDLES
- 1 pair 3.25mm (USA 3) (UK 10)
- 1 pair 3.75mm (USA 5) (UK 9)
- 1 pair 4.00mm (USA 6) (UK 8)
- 3.25mm circular needle (USA 3) (UK 10) or a set of double-pointed needles

TENSION
22.5 sts and 30 rows to 10cm, measured over stockinette stitch using 4.00mm needles.

YARN
Jo Sharp 8-ply DK Pure-Wool Handknitting Yarn

	Key		Color	Quantity			
				S	(M	L)	
Woman's	1		Indigo 305	11	12	12	x 50g
Sweater	2	■	Navy 327	4	4	4	x 50g
	3		Gold 320	1	1	1	x 50g
	4	⊡	Naples 321	1	1	1	x 50g
	5	▨	Ginger 322	2	2	2	x 50g
	6		Ruby 326	1	1	1	x 50g
Man's	1		Black 302	13	14	14	x 50g
Sweater	2	■	Indigo 305	4	4	4	x 50g
	3		Gold 320	1	1	1	x 50g
	4	⊡	Antique 323	1	1	1	x 50g
	5	▨	Ginger 322	2	2	2	x 50g
	6		Ruby 326	1	1	1	x 50g
				3-5	(6-8) yo		
Child's	1		Indigo 305	7	8		x 50g
Sweater	2	■	Navy 327	2	2		x 50g
	3		Gold 320	1	1		x 50g
	4	⊡	Naples 321	1	1		x 50g
	5	▨	Ginger 322	1	1		x 50g
	6		Ruby 326	1	1		x 50g

Woman's and Man's Sweater

BACK
Using 3.75mm needles and col 1, cast on 136 (144, 152) sts, then joining in col 2, cont in k2, p2 two-col rib as follows:

Row 1 On rs, [k2 col 2, p2 col 1], rep to end.

Row 2 On ws, [k2 col 1, p2 col 2], rep to end.
Rep these 2 rows 9 times [20 rows].
Change to 4.00mm needles. Using st st, beg with a k row, foll graph on p. 52 for col changes.* Work 178 (182, 186) rows.

Shape shoulders Cast off 9 (10, 11) sts at beg of next 8 rows and 10 (10, 10) st at beg of foll 2 rows. Leave rem 44 sts on a holder.

FRONT
Work as given for back to *. Work 166 (170, 174) rows.

Shape front neck Patt 55 (59, 63) sts, turn, and leave rem sts on a holder. Work each side of neck separately. Cast off 2 sts at neck edge on next and foll alt rows 3 times, and 1 st on foll alt rows 3 times.

Shape shoulders Cast off 9 (10, 11) sts at beg of next and foll alt rows 4 times. Work 1 row. Cast off rem 10 sts. With rs facing, leave 26 sts on a holder. Rejoin yarn to rem sts and complete second side to match first side, rev all shaping.

SLEEVES
Man's sleeve shown in ( ).
Using 3.25mm needles and col 1, cast on 56 (62) sts.
Woman's version: Join in col 2 and work in two-col rib, as given for back.
Man's version: Work in k2, p2 rib.
Work 19 (19) rows ending with a rs row.

SLEEVES

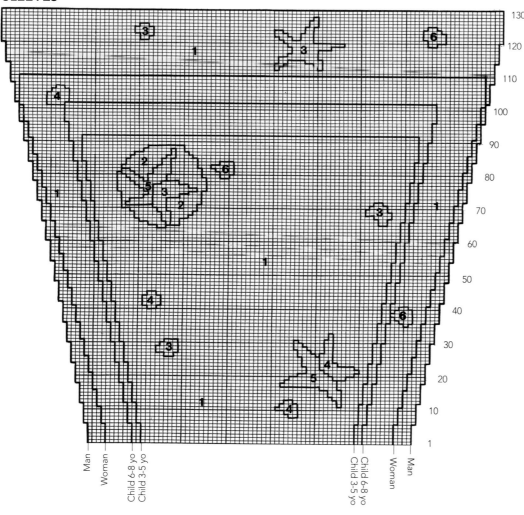

Next row (inc) Rib 8 (6), m1, [rib 5, m1] 8 (10) times, rib 8 (6) [65 (73) sts]. Change to 4.00mm needles. Using st st, beg with a k row, foll graph above for col changes. AT THE SAME TIME, shape sides by inc 1 st at each end of 7 (7)th row and every foll 5 (6)th row, 19 (19) times [105 (113) sts]. Work 8 (9) rows [110 (130) rows]. Cast off loosely and evenly.

MAKING UP

Press all pieces, except ribbing, gently on ws using a warm iron over a damp cloth. Using backstitch, join shoulder seams. Center sleeves and join. Join side and sleeve seams using edge-to-edge stitch on ribs.**

Neckband Using 3.25mm circular needle and cols 1 and 2, with rs facing, pick up and k2 col 1, k2 col 2, 27 sts down left side front neck; 26 sts from st holder across front neck; 27 sts up right side front neck; and 44 sts from st holder across back of neck (124 sts). Work 4.5cm in k2, p2 two-col rib, as given for back, working in rounds. Using col 1, cast off evenly in rib. Press seams.

Woman's, man's sweater

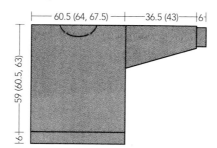

CHILD'S BACK & FRONT

	3-5 yo
6-8 yo	

	3-5 yo
	6-8 yo

Child's Sweater

BACK

Using 3.75mm needles and col 1, cast on 100 (106) sts. Then joining in col 2, cont in k2, p2 two-col rib as follows:

Row 1 On rs, [k2 col 2, p2 col 1], rep to end.

Row 2 On ws, [p2 col 2, k2 col 1], rep to end. Rep these 2 rows 6 times [14 rows]. Change to 4.00mm needles. Using st st, beg with a k row, foll graph above for col changes.* Work 126 (132) rows.

Shape shoulders Cast off 8 (9) sts at beg of next 6 rows, then 9 (9) sts at beg of foll 2 rows. Leave rem 34 sts on a holder.

FRONT

Work as back to *. Work 116 (122) rows.

Shape front neck Work 40 (43) sts, turn, and leave rem sts on a holder. Work each side of neck separately. Dec 1 st at neck edge on next and foll rows 7 times [33 (36 sts)]. Work 2 rows.

Shape shoulders Cast off 8 (9) sts at beg of next and foll alt rows 3 times. Work 1 row. Cast off rem 9 (9) sts.

With rs facing, leave 20 (20) sts on a holder. Rejoin yarn to rem sts and complete second side to match first.

SLEEVES

Using 3.25mm needles and col 1, cast on 40 (44) sts. Join in col 2 and work 11 rows in two-col rib, as given for back, ending with a rs row.

Next row (inc) Rib 3 (5), m1, [rib 5 (5), m1] 7 times, rib 2 (4) [48 (52) sts].
Change to 4.00mm needles. Using st st, beg with a k row, foll graph on p. 53 for col changes. AT THE SAME TIME, shape sides by inc 1 st at each end of 7 (7)th row and foll 6 (6)th rows 13 (15) times [76 (84) sts]. Work 7 (5) rows [92 (102) rows]. Cast off loosely and evenly.

MAKING UP

Refer to woman's and man's sweater "making up" to **.

Neckband Using 3.25mm circular needle and cols 1 and 2, with rs facing, pick up and k2 col 1, k2 col 2, 21 sts down left side front neck; 20 sts from st holder across front neck; 21 sts up right side front neck; and 34 sts from st holder across back of neck [96 sts]. Work 3cm in k2, p2 two-col rib, as given for back, working in rounds. Using col 1, cast off evenly in rib. Press seams.

Child's sweater

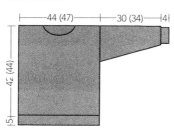

HEIRLOOM

WOMAN'S JACKET

The Heirloom jacket features woven-stitched sleeves and collar and has side seam pockets. This pattern is suitable for an experienced knitter with knowledge of intarsia knitting (see instructions on pp. 7-8).

NEEDLES
- I pair 3.25mm (USA 3) (UK 10)
- I pair 4.00mm (USA 6) (UK 8)
- I pair 5.00mm (USA 8) (UK 6)

BUTTONS
Ten 1.5cm

TENSION
22.5 sts and 30 rows to 10cm, measured over patterned stockinette stitch using 4.00mm needles; and 26 sts and 44 rows to 10cm, measured over woven stitch pattern using 5.00mm needles.

WOVEN STITCH PATTERN
Using an uneven number of stitches.
Row I On rs, kI, *yf, slI purlwise, yb, kI, rep from * to end.
Row 2 P2, *yb, slI purlwise, yf, pI, rep from * to last st, pI. Rep these two rows.

YARN
Jo Sharp 8-ply DK Pure-Wool Handknitting Yarn

Key		Color	Quantity	
1	⊡	Black 302	15	x 50g
2	☑	Earth 334	2	x 50g
3	☑	Brick 333	2	x 50g
4	☒	Wine 307	2	x 50g
5	☑	Violet 319	2	x 50g
6	☒	Ginger 322	1	x 50g
7		Gold 320	1	x 50g
8		Olive 313	1	x 50g
9		Mosaic 336	1	x 50g
O		Renaissance 312	1	x 50g
A		Naples 321	1	x 50g
U		Wedgewood 340	1	x 50g

BACK
Using 4.00mm needles and col 1, cast on 132 sts. Using st st, beg with a k row, foll graph on p. 58 for col changes. Work 204 rows.

Shape shoulders Cast off 8 sts at beg of next 12 rows. Cast off rem 36 sts.

LEFT FRONT
Using 4.00mm needles and col 1, cast on 66 sts. Using st st, beg with a k row, foll graph on p. 58 for col changes. Work 108 rows.

Shape front neck Dec 1 st at neck edge on next row and every foll 4th row 4 times, then on foll 6th rows 13 times (48 sts). Work 1 row.

Shape shoulder Cast off 8 sts at beg of next and foll alt rows 5 times in all. Work 1 row. Cast off rem 8 sts.

RIGHT FRONT
Work as given for left front, foll graph on p. 58 for right front col changes and rev all shaping.

SLEEVES
Using 5.00mm needles and col 1, cast on 71 sts. Using woven st patt, work 44 rows. Cont in patt. AT THE SAME TIME, shape sides by inc 1 st at each end of next row and every foll alt row 18 times, then every foll 4th row 30 times (169 sts), noting to take sts made into patt. Work 5 rows. Cast off loosely and evenly.

POCKET LININGS (MAKE 2)
Using 4.00mm needles and col 1, cast on 33 sts. Work 62 rows st st. Cast off.

MAKING UP
On ws, gently press back and fronts only, using a warm iron over a damp cloth. Using backstitch, join shoulder seams. Center sleeves and join, using edge-to-edge stitch for first 44 rows at cuff edge. Join sleeve seams. Fold cuffs back for 5cm.

Right front ┬ Left front
Back

Back lower band With rs facing and using 4.00mm needles and col 1, pick up and k 153 sts evenly along lower edge of back. Change to 5.00mm needles, and work 5cm in woven st patt, beg and ending with a 2nd row. Cast off evenly in k1, p1 rib, using 3.25mm needles.

Left front lower band With rs facing and using 4.00mm needles and col 1, pick up and k 75 sts evenly along lower edge of left front. Complete as given for back lower band.

Right front lower band Work as given for left front lower band. Sl st rs of pocket linings to ws of fronts on 3 sides, placing cast-on edge of lining to top (pick up edge) of lower band and 62 rows along side edge of front, leaving this side edge open. Using backstitch, join side seams, stitching both pocket lining and front to back for first 20 rows above lower band, then pocket lining only to back for next 42 rows, then fronts to back for rem.

Pocket edgings With rs facing and using 4.00mm needles and col 1, pick up and k 39 sts evenly along side edge (pocket) opening on fronts. Change to 5.00mm needles, and work 5 rows woven st patt, beg with a 2nd row. Cast off evenly in k1, p1 rib, using 3.25mm needles. Sl st sides of pocket edgings into position, over-lapping back.

Front bands and collar Using 5.00mm needles and col 1, cast on 15 sts. Work 179 rows woven st patt.

Shape for collar Keeping patt correct, inc 1 st at beg of next row (ws) and every foll 8th row, 19 times (35 sts). *Shape for back of collar:* When turning, bring yarn to front of work, slip next st onto right-hand needle, take yarn back, then turn and proceed as instructed. This avoids holes in work.

Row 1 On rs, patt 21, turn.

Row 2 Patt to end. Work 16 rows patt across all 35 sts. Rep last 18 rows 3 times, then rows 1 and 2 again. Work 1 row. Dec 1 st at beg of next row (ws) and every foll 8th row 19 times (15 sts). Work 44 rows patt.

Place buttonholes—row 1 On rs, k1, yft, sl1 purlwise, ybk, k1, cast off next 2 sts, (k1, yft, sl1 purlwise, ybk) twice, cast off next 2 sts, yft, sl1 purlwise, ybk, k1.

Row 2 P2, (p into front, then back, then front) of next st, (p1, ybk, sl1 purlwise, yft) twice, (p into front, then back, then front) of next st, ybk, sl1 purlwise, p2 (2 buttonholes). Work 30 rows patt. Rep last 32 rows 3 times, then rows 1 and 2 again (10 buttonholes in all). Work 6 rows patt. Cast off evenly in k1, p1 rib, using 3.25mm needles.
Using edge-to-edge stitch, attach shaped edge of collar and front bands to jacket by placing ws to rs of jacket and buttonhole band to right front. Fold collar outward so that rs of patt now faces. Sew buttons on to correspond with buttonholes. Press seams.

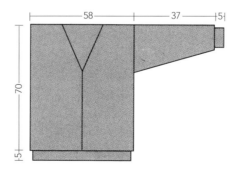

WOVEN WAISTCOAT

WOMAN'S VEST

The Woven Waistcoat uses the woven stitch. This pattern is easy to follow and is suitable for a beginner knitter.

NEEDLES
• I pair 4.5mm (USA 7) (UK 7)

BUTTONS
Version I—Five 1.5cm
Version 2—Four 1.5cm

TENSION
27 sts and 46 rows to 10cm, measured over woven stitch pattern using 4.5mm needles.

WOVEN STITCH
Use an uneven number of stitches.
Row I On rs, kI, *yf, slI purlwise, yb, kI. Rep from * to end.
Row 2 On ws, p2, *yb, slI purlwise, yf, pI. Rep from * to last stitch, pI.
Rep these two rows.

YARN
Jo Sharp 8-ply DK Pure-Wool Handknitting Yarn

	Key	Color	Quantity	
VERSION 1	1	Antique 323	5	x 50g
VERSION 2	1	Wine 307	4	x 50g
	2	Brick 333	1	x 50g
	3	Chartreuse 330	1	x 50g
	4	Jade 316	1	x 50g
	5	Lemon 308	1	x 50g
	6	Violet 319	1	x 50g
	7	Gold 320	1	x 50g

Increasing when using woven stitch
When inc at beg of row:
• If first st is a k st, kfb into this st.
• If first st is a p st, pbf into this st.
When inc at end of row, work to last two sts, then:
• If last but one st is a k st in woven stitch, kfb into this st.
• If last but one st is a p st in woven stitch, pbf into this st.
• If last but one st is a sl st in woven stitch, slip this st, then mI.

Version 1
(Shown in photo on p. 61 at right.)

BACK
Using 4.5mm needles and col 1, cast on 107 (115, 123) sts. Working in woven stitch throughout, inc 1 st at each end of 13th row and every foll 12th row 5 times [119 (127, 135) sts]. Cont without further shaping for 19 (23, 27) rows [92 (96, 100) rows]. (Adjust length here if required.)

Shape armholes Cast off 2 sts at beg of next 4 rows, then dec 1 st at each end of the next and foll alt rows 7 times, then every 4th row 5 times [87 (95, 103) sts]. Cont without further shaping for 65 (73, 81) rows [194 (206, 218) rows].

Shape shoulders Cast off 2 sts at beg of next 14 (16, 18) rows [59 (63, 67) sts].

Shape neck Cast off 2 sts, work 16 sts, leave rem 41 (45, 49) sts on holder. Cast off 2 sts at beg (neck edge) of next and foll ws rows. AT THE SAME TIME, cast off 2 sts at beg and 1 st at end (neck edge) of rs rows, until 1 st rem. Cast off.

Join yarn to sts on holder and cast off 23 (27, 31) sts in woven stitch. Work 18 rem sts, turn, and cast off 2 sts at beg and 1 st at end (neck edge) of next and foll alt rows (ws). AT THE SAME TIME, cast off 2 sts at beg (neck edge) of rs rows, until 3 sts rem. Cast off.

LEFT FRONT

Using 4.5mm needles and col 1, cast on 3 sts. (Note: Thumb-method cast-on will give a neater finish to peaks.)

Row 1 On ws, p3.

Row 2 K1, yf, sl1 purlwise, yb, m1, k1.

Row 3 P1, yb, sl1 purlwise, yf, pbf, p1.

Row 4 K2, yf, sl1 purlwise, yb, kfb, k1.

Row 5 P1, *p1, yb, sl1 purlwise, yf, rep from * to last st, m1, p1.

Row 6 *K1, yf, sl1 purlwise, yb, rep from * to last st, m1, k1.

Row 7 *P1, yb, sl1 purlwise, yf, rep from * to last 2 sts, pbf, p1.

Row 8 K1, *k1, yf, sl1 purlwise, yb, rep from * to last 2 sts, kfb, k1.
Rep rows 5 to 8 until there are 34 sts, **then inc 1 st at end of ws rows as before and 1 st at each end of rs rows until there are 47 (50, 53) sts, taking care to keep woven-stitch pattern correct. Keeping front edge straight, inc 1 st at beg of rs row and 2 sts at end of ws row (1 st as before and then pbf in last st) until there are 65 (68, 71) sts. Cont to keep front edge straight, inc 1 st at beg of 13th row and every foll 12th row 5 times [71 (74, 77) sts]. Cont without further shaping for 19 (23, 27) rows (adjust length here if required).

Shape armhole and neck Cast off 4 sts at beg of next row (rs), 2 sts at beg of foll alt rows 5 times, and 1 st at beg of foll alt rows 6 times. AT THE SAME TIME, dec 1 st at end (neck edge) of these rs rows 12 times [39 (42, 45) sts]. Keeping armhole edge straight, dec 1 st on neck edge of every foll 4th row 17 (18, 19) times [22 (24, 26) sts]. Cont without further shaping for 11 (15, 19) rows.

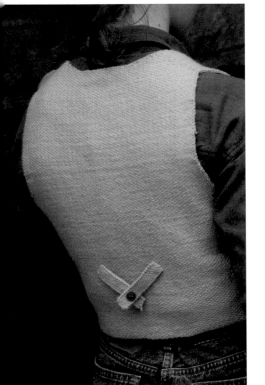

Shape shoulder With rs facing, cast off 2 sts at beg of next and alt rows until 2 sts rem. Work 1 row. K rem 2 sts tog.

RIGHT FRONT

Work as for left front until **, then cont as for left front, rev all shaping, as follows. Inc 1 st each end of ws rows and 1 st at end of rs rows, until there are 48 (51, 54) sts, ending with a ws row. Keeping front edge straight, inc 2 sts at end of rs row and 1 st at beg of ws row until there are 65 (68, 71) sts. AT THE SAME TIME, make first buttonhole when straight front edge measures approx 1cm.

Buttonhole row 1 K1, sl1, k1, sl1, cast off 3 sts, work to end, keeping inc correct at side edge.

Buttonhole row 2 Work to buttonhole, cast on 3 sts, p1, sl 1, p2. Cont to match left front, inc 1 st at end of 14th row and every foll 12th row 5 times [71 (74, 77) sts]. Cont without further shaping for 19 (23, 27) rows (adjust length here if required), making 3 more buttonholes, the last to come 1cm from start of neck shaping and the other two spaced evenly between this and the first buttonhole.

Shape armhole and neck Dec 1 st at beg (neck edge) of next and foll alt rows 12 times. AT THE SAME TIME, cast off 4 sts at beg of next ws row, then 2 sts at beg of foll alt rows 5 times, then 1 st at beg of foll alt rows 6 times [39 (42, 45) sts]. Work 2 rows. Keeping armhole edge straight, dec 1 st at beg (neck edge) of next and every foll 4th row until 22 (24, 26) sts rem. Cont without further shaping for 12 (16, 20) rows.

Shape shoulder With ws facing, cast off 2 sts at beg of next and alt rows until 2 sts rem. Work 1 row. K rem 2 sts tog.

BACK TABS (MAKE 2)

Using 4.5mm needles and col 1, cast on 7 sts and work 38 rows in woven stitch. Cast off.

MAKING UP

Press all pieces gently on ws using a warm iron over a damp cloth. Using backstitch, join shoulder seams and side seams. Sew on 4 buttons to correspond with buttonholes.*** Secure tabs at back, joining the two with a button (see photo at left).

Version 2

(Shown in photo at right.)

BACK
Work as for Version 1.

LEFT FRONT
Work as for Version 1 using the foll col
sequence:
3 rows col 1.
*1 row col 2.
1 row col 3.
1 row col 4.
1 row col 5.
1 row col 6.
1 row col 7.
1 row col 1.
1 row col 2.
1 row col 3.
1 row col 4.
1 row col 7.
1 row col 3.
1 row col 2.
2 rows col 1.
1 row col 6.
2 rows col 4.
1 row col 6.
1 row col 2.
1 row col 3.
1 row col 7.
1 row col 2.
1 row col 3.
1 row col 7.
2 rows col 2.
1 row col 1.
1 row col 4.
2 rows col 6.
1 row col 7.
1 row col 1.
Rep from * for 33-row col sequence.

RIGHT FRONT
Pattern as per Version 1, using Version 2 left
front col sequence.

FRONT TABS (MAKE 2)
Using 4.5mm needles and col 1, cast on 9 sts
and work 38 rows in woven stitch. Cast off.

MAKING UP
Refer to Version 1 "making up" to ***. Center
front tabs approximately 12cm from bottom of
front peaks, and sew into position.

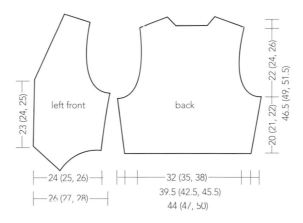

JESSICA

WOMAN'S SWEATER

This drop-shouldered, cropped sweater features snug-fitting, elongated wristbands and waistband and a simple repeat texture in the bodice. The pattern is suitable for a beginner knitter.

NEEDLES
- 1 pair 3.75mm (USA 5) (UK 9)
- 1 pair 4.00mm (USA 6) (UK 8)
- 3.75mm circular needle (USA 5) (UK 9) or a set of double-pointed needles

TENSION
22.5 sts and 30 rows to 10cm using 4.00mm needles.

YARN
Jo Sharp 8-ply DK Pure-Wool Handknitting Yarn

Key	Color	Quantity			
		S	(M	L)	
1	Wine 307	12	12	12	x 50g
2	Jade 316	1	1	1	x 50g

BACK
Using 3.75mm needles and col 2, cast on 134 (142, 150) sts.

Row 1 On rs, k2, *p2, k2, rep from * to end.

Row 2 On ws, p2, *k2, p2, rep from * to end. Change to col 1, and rep rows 1 and 2 until band measures 15cm, ending with a ws row. Change to 4.00mm needles, and foll graph on pp. 66-67 for texture patt. Work ** 106 rows (adjust length here, if desired). Cast off.

FRONT
Work as given for back to **. Work 84 rows (adjust length here, if desired).

Shape front neck Work 55 (59, 63) sts, turn, and leave rem sts on a st holder. Work each side of neck separately. Cast off 2 sts at neck edge on next row and foll alt rows twice, and 1 st on foll alt rows 3 times [46 (50, 54) sts]. Work 10 rows. Cast off.
With rs facing, leave 24 sts on a st holder, rejoin yarn to rem sts, and complete second side to match first side, rev all shaping.

SLEEVES
Using 3.75mm needles and col 2, cast on 54 sts.

Row 1 On rs, k2, *p2, k2, rep from * to end.

Row 2 On ws, p2, *k2, p2, rep from * to end. Change to col 1, and rep rows 1 and 2 until band measures 15cm, ending with a rs row.

Next row (inc) Rib 2, *m1, rib 5, rep from * 9 times, m1, rib 2 [65 sts]. Change to 4.00mm needles, and foll graph on pp. 66-67 for texture

FRONT, BACK & SLEEVE

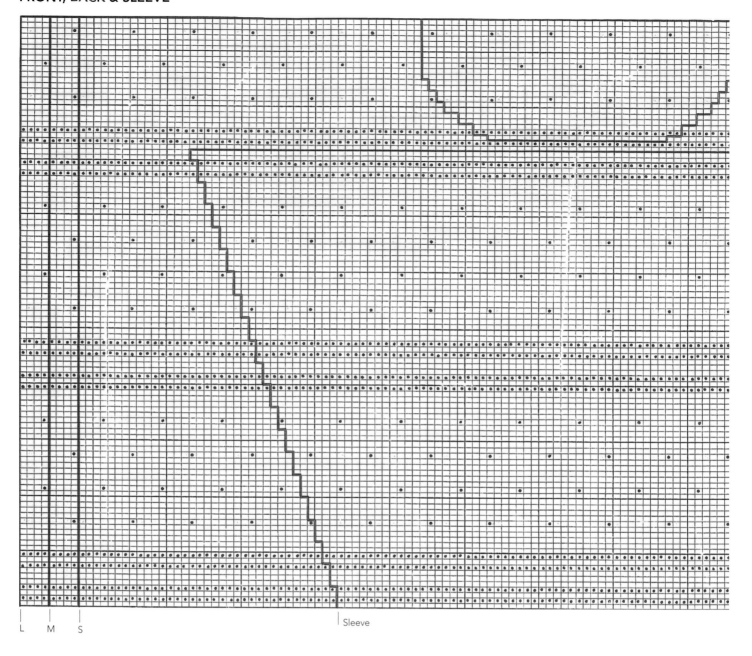

 L M S

Sleeve

patt. AT THE SAME TIME, shape sides by inc 1 st at each end of 5th row and every foll 4th row 19 times [105 sts]. Work 1 row [82 rows] or until length desired. Cast off loosely and evenly.

MAKING UP

Press all pieces, except ribbing, gently on ws using a warm iron over a damp cloth. Using backstitch, join shoulder seams. Center sleeves and join. Join side and sleeve seams using edge-to-edge stitch on ribs.

Neckband With rs facing and using a 3.75mm circular needle and col 1, pick up and k 28 sts down left side front neck; 24 sts from st holder at center front; 28 sts up right side front neck; and 44 sts across back neck (124 sts). Work in k2, p2 rib for 10 rounds. Change to col 2, and cont in rib for 2 rounds. Cast off in col 2. Press seams.

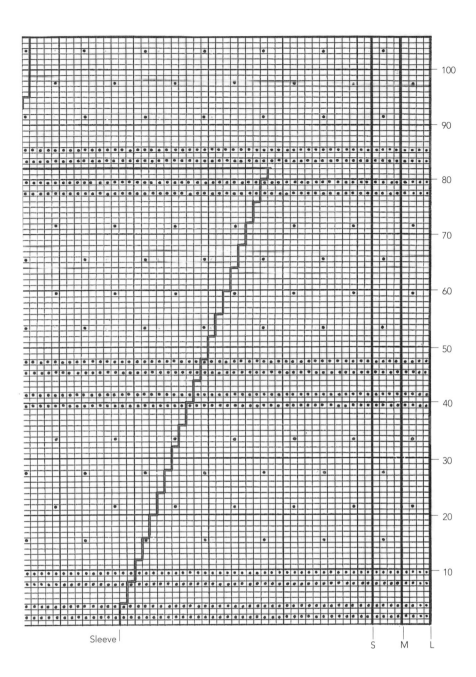

Sleeve

S M L

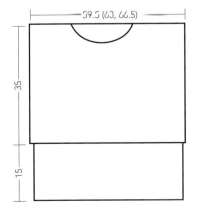

59.5 (63, 66.5)

35

15

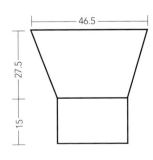

46.5

27.5

15

KAZAK

WOMAN'S CARDIGAN

This pattern is suitable for an experienced knitter with knowledge of intarsia knitting (see instructions on pp. 7-8). This cardigan is loose fitting and drop shouldered. The longer version has set-in pockets.

NEEDLES
- 1 pair 3.75mm (USA 5) (UK 9)
- 1 pair 4.00mm (USA 6) (UK 8)

BUTTONS
Short version—Four 2cm

Long version—Five 2cm

TENSION
22.5 sts and 30 rows to 10cm, measured over patterned stockinette stitch using 4.00mm needles.

YARN
Jo Sharp 8-ply DK Pure-Wool Handknitting Yarn

Key		Color	Quantity			
			S	(M	L)	
SHORT VERSION						
1	☐	Mosaic 336	11	12	12	x 50g
2	◉	Jade 316	1	1	1	x 50g
3	☐	Violet 319	1	1	1	x 50g
4	⊡	Navy 327	2	2	2	x 50g
5	▽	Forest 318	1	1	1	x 50g
6	◨	Terracotta 332	1	1	1	x 50g
7	⊠	Brick 333	1	1	1	x 50g
8	⊡	Wine 307	1	1	1	x 50g
LONG VERSION						
1	☐	Navy 327	14	15	15	x 50g
2	◉	Slate 328	1	1	1	x 50g
3	☐	Coral 304	2	2	2	x 50g
4	⊡	Cherry 309	3	3	3	x 50g
5	▽	Wine 307	2	2	2	x 50g
6	◨	Gold 320	2	2	2	x 50g
7	⊠	Violet 319	2	2	2	x 50g
8	⊡	Olive 313	1	1	1	x 50g

Short Version

BACK

Using 3.75mm needles and col 1, cast on 130 (138, 146) sts. Work 9cm in k1, p1 rib, ending with a ws row. Change to 4.00mm needles. Using st st, beg with a k row, foll graph on p. 70 (commencing on row 75) for col changes. Work 122 (126, 130) rows.

Shape shoulders Cast off 8 (9, 10) sts at beg of next 10 rows. Cast off rem 50 (48, 46) sts.

LEFT FRONT

Using 3.75mm needles and col 1, cast on 64 (68, 72) sts. Work in k1, p1 rib as per back. Change to 4.00mm needles. Using st st, beg with a k row, foll graph on p. 70 (commencing on row 75) for col changes. Work 60 (64, 68) rows.

Shape front neck Keeping armhole edge straight, dec 1 st at neck edge on next row and every foll 4th row, until there are 48 (52, 56) sts. Work 1 row.

Shape shoulders Cast off 8 (9, 10) sts at beg of next and foll alt rows 5 times. Work 1 row. Cast off rem 8 (7, 6) sts.

RIGHT FRONT

Work as given for left front, rev all shaping, and foll graph on p. 70 for right front col changes.

SLEEVES

Using 3.75mm needles and col 1, cast on 54 sts. Work 8cm in k1, p1 rib, ending with a rs row.

Next row [inc] Rib 2, [m1, rib 5] 10 times, m1, rib 2 [65 sts]. Change to 4.00mm needles. Using st st, beg with a k row, foll graph on p. 71 for col changes. AT THE SAME TIME, shape sides by

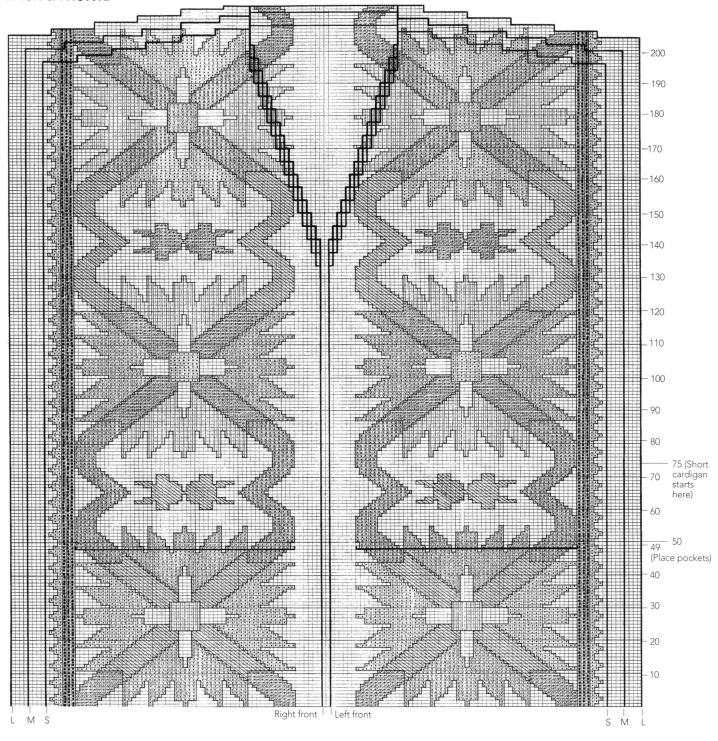

inc 1 st at each end of 7th row and foll 6th row 10 times, then foll 4th row 9 times [105 sts], taking extra sts into patt as they occur. Work 5 rows [108 rows]. Cast off loosely and evenly.

MAKING UP
Press all pieces, except ribbing, gently on ws using a warm iron over a damp cloth. Using backstitch, join shoulder seams. Center sleeves

and join. Join side and sleeve seams using edge-to-edge stitch on ribs.

Collar Using 4.00mm needles and col 4, cast on 182 sts.

Row 1 * K2, p2, rep from * to last 2 sts, k2.

Row 2 * P2, k2, rep from * to last 2 sts, p2. Change to col 1 and cont in k2, p2 rib for 6 rows.

SLEEVE

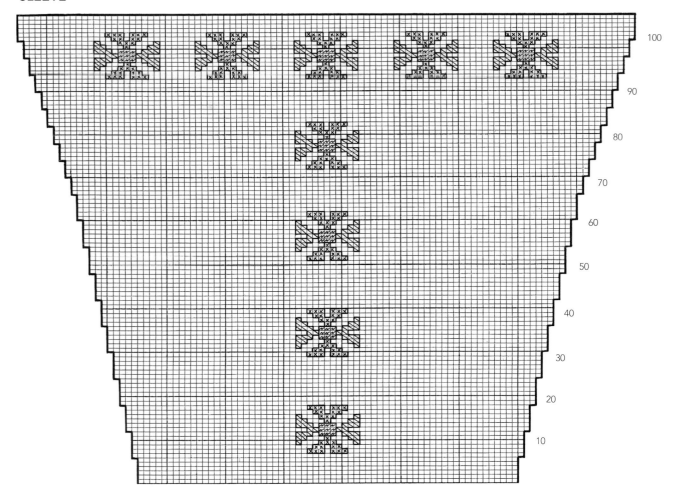

Cast off 3 sts at beg of next 14 rows, then 4 sts at beg of next 22 rows, keeping rib patt correct [52 sts]. Cast off evenly in rib as set. Using edge-to-edge stitch, attach cast-off edge of collar piece to neckhole.**

Button band With rs facing and using 3.75mm needles and col 1, pick up and k 70 (74, 76) sts evenly along left front from bottom edge to beg of neck shaping. Work 6 rows in k2, p2 rib. Change to col 4, and work a further 2 rows in rib as set. Cast off evenly in rib. Mark position on button band for 4 buttons, the first to come 2cm up from lower edge, the last to come 2cm down from top edge, and the remainder spaced evenly between. Sew on buttons.

Buttonhole band Work as for button band, making buttonholes to correspond with position of buttons. Press seams.

Long Version

BACK

Using 3.75mm needles and col 1, cast on 130 (138, 146) sts. Work 9cm in k1, p1 rib, ending with a ws row. Change to 4.00mm needles. Using st st, beg with a k row, and foll graph on p. 70 for col changes. Work 196 (200, 204) rows.

Shape shoulders Cast off 8 (9, 10) sts at beg of next 10 rows. Cast off rem 50 (48, 46) sts.

POCKET LINING (MAKE 2)

Using 4.00mm needles and col 1, cast on 51 sts. Work 47 rows in st st, beg with a k row. Leave sts on a holder.

LEFT FRONT

Using 3.75mm needles, cast on 64 (68, 72) sts. Work k1, p1 rib as per back. Change to 4.00mm needles. Using st st, beg with a k row, and foll

graph on p. 70 for col changes. Work 48 rows, ending with a ws row.*

Row 49—Place pocket lining Patt 7 (11, 15) sts, slip next 51 sts onto a holder, and in place of these, patt across 51 sts of first pocket lining, patt 6 (6, 6). Cont in patt until 134 (138, 142) patt rows completed.

Shape front neck Keeping armhole edge straight, dec 1 st at neck edge on next row and every foll 4th row, until there are 48 (52, 56) sts. Work 1 row.

Shape shoulders Cast off 8 (9, 10) sts at beg of next and foll alt rows 5 times. Work 1 row. Cast off rem 8 (7, 6) sts.

RIGHT FRONT
Work as given for left front to *, foll graph on p. 70 for right front col changes.

Row 49 —Place pocket lining Patt 6 (6, 6) sts, slip next 51 sts onto a st holder, and in place of these, patt across sts of 2nd pocket lining, patt 7 (11, 15). Cont as given for left front, rev all shaping and foll graph on p. 70 for right front col changes.

SLEEVES
Work as per short version sleeve.

MAKING UP
Work as per short version "making up" to **.

Button band With rs facing and using 3.75mm needles and col 1, pick up and k 118 (122, 124) sts evenly along left front from bottom edge to beg of neck shaping. Work 6 rows in k2, p2 rib. Change to col 4, and work a further 2 rows in rib as set. Cast off evenly in rib. Mark position on button band for 5 buttons, the first to come 2cm up from lower edge, the last to come 2cm down from top edge, and the remainder spaced evenly between. Sew on buttons.

Buttonhole band Work as for button band, making buttonholes to correspond with position of buttons.

Pocket tops With rs facing and 3.75mm needles, work 8 rows k1, p1 rib across sts left on holder, foll graph on p. 70 for col changes. Cast off evenly in rib.
Sew pocket linings into place on ws, and finish off pocket tops on rs. Press seams.

Short cardigan

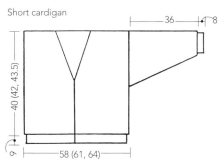

36 | 8

40 (42, 43.5)

9

58 (61, 64)

Long cardigan

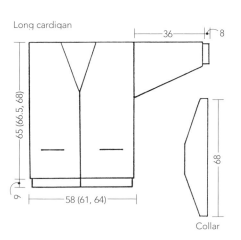

36 | 8

65 (66.5, 68)

68

9

58 (61, 64)

Collar

CHEQUER

MAN'S AND CHILD'S SWEATER, WOMAN'S, MAN'S, AND CHILD'S CARDIGAN

These patterns are for simple, drop-shouldered sweaters or cardigans, with sizes to fit men, women, boys, and girls. The 7 designs range in color complexity (version 1 being the simplest, to version 7, the most complex). They give beginner knitters an introduction to intarsia or picture knitting (see instructions on pp. 7-8) and provide an easy start toward developing color-joining skills.

NEEDLES
- I pair 3.75mm (USA 5) (UK 9)
- I pair 4.00mm (USA 6) (UK 8)
- 3.75mm circular needle (USA 5) (UK 9) or a set of double-pointed needles

BUTTONS
Woman's and man's cardigan—Six 2.5cm
Child's cardigan—Four 2cm or five 1.5cm (optional)

TENSION
22.5 sts and 30 rows to 10cm, measured over stockinette stitch using 4.00mm needles.

Man's Sweater
Note: Refer to version you are knitting for colors required.

BACK
Using 3.75mm needles, cast on 134 (142, 150) sts. Work in k1, p1 rib for 26 rows. Change to 4.00mm needles. Using st st, beg with a k row, foll graph on p. 77 for col changes.* Work 190 rows. Cast off.

FRONT
Work as given for back to *. Work 168 rows.

Shape front neck Work 55 (59, 63) sts, turn, and leave rem sts on a holder. Work each side of neck separately. Cast off 2 sts at neck edge on

YARN

Jo Sharp 8-ply DK Pure-Wool Handknitting Yarn

VERSION 1

No.	Color	Graph key	Quantity S	(M)	L)	
1	Mulberry 325	A B C G H K M P Q T U W Z	7	8	8	x 50g
2	Violet 319	O X	3	4	4	x 50g
3	Forest 318	D E F J L N R S V Y	5	5	5	x 50g

VERSION 2

No.	Color	Graph key	Quantity 3-5	(6-8) yo	
1	Ruby 326	A F G J K L M U X Z	5	5	x 50g
2	Navy 327	C E H O V W Y	2	2	x 50g
3	Ginger 322	B Q R S	2	2	x 50g
4	Forest 318	D N P T	2	2	x 50g

VERSION 3

No.	Color	Graph key	Quantity S	(M)	L)	
1	Wine 307	A F G J K L M O U X Z	11	11	11	x 50g
2	Ruby 326	C E H V W Y	3	3	3	x 50g
3	Smoke 339	D N P T	2	3	3	x 50g
4	Forest 318	R B	2	2	2	x 50g
5	Jade 316	S Q	1	1	2	x 50g

VERSION 4

No.	Color	Graph key	Quantity 3-5	(6-8) yo	
1	Navy 327	A C D G H N R S U W Z	5	5	x 50g
2	Jade 316	B K P Q T	2	2	x 50g
3	Violet 319	M O X	2	2	x 50g
4	Forest 318	E F J L V Y	2	2	x 50g

VERSION 5

No.	Color	Graph key	Quantity S	(M)	L)	
1	Navy 327	G O X	9	9	9	x 50g
2	Jade 316	A C	1	1	1	x 50g
3	Wine 307	B F H K Q R S V W Y	4	5	5	x 50g
4	Violet 319	D E J L M N P T U Z	4	5	5	x 50g

VERSION 6

No.	Color	Graph key	Quantity 3-5	(6-8) yo	
1	Mosaic 336	B G R Y W	4	5	x 50g
2	Jade 316	C D N P T	2	2	x 50g
3	Satin 311	E K L O X Z	2	3	x 50g
4	Violet 319	H J M U V	2	2	x 50g
5	Wedgewood 340	A F S Q	1	1	x 50g

VERSION 7

No.	Color	Graph key	Quantity S	(M)	L)	
1	Smoke 339	G O W Y	8	8	8	x 50g
2	Jacaranda 314	E F	1	1	1	x 50g
3	Lilac 324	J L M U Z	3	3	3	x 50g
4	Navy 327	H V X	4	4	4	x 50g
5	Violet 319	D K N P T	4	4	4	x 50g
6	Wedgewood 340	A C	1	1	1	x 50g
7	Forest 318	B Q R S	3	3	3	x 50g

SLEEVES

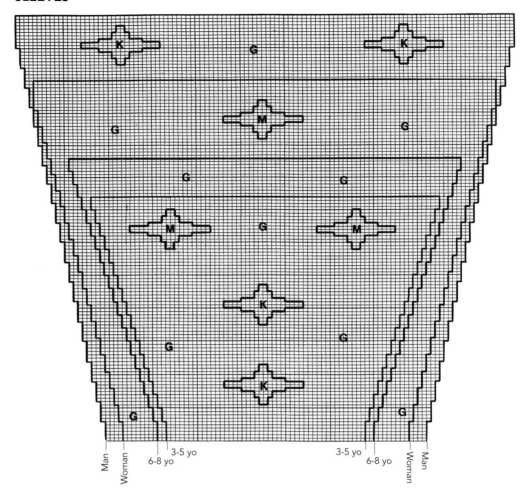

next row and foll alt rows, twice, and 1 st on foll alt rows, 3 times [46 (50, 54) sts]. Work 10 rows. Cast off.

With rs facing, leave 24 sts on a holder, rejoin yarn to rem sts and complete second side to match first side, rev all shaping.

SLEEVES

Note: man's sleeve is shown in ( ).
Using 3.75mm needles, cast on 54 (62) sts. Work in k1, p1 rib for 19 (25) rows, ending with a rs row.

Next row (inc) Rib 2 (6), *m1, rib 5, rep from * 10 times, m1, rib 2 (6) [65 (73) sts].
Change to 4.00mm needles. Using st st, beg with a k row, foll graph above for col changes. AT THE SAME TIME, shape sides by inc 1 st at each end of 7 (7)th row and every foll 5 (6)th row, 19 (19) times [105 (113) sts]. Work 8 (9) rows [110 (130) rows]. Cast off loosely and evenly.

MAKING UP

Press all pieces, except ribbing, gently on ws using a warm iron over a damp cloth. Using backstitch, join shoulder seams. Center sleeves and join. Join side and sleeve seams using edge-to-edge stitch on ribs.**

Neckband Using a 3.75mm circular needle, with rs facing, pick up and k 28 sts down left side front neck; 24 sts from holder at center front; 28 sts up right side front neck; and 44 sts across back neck (124 sts). Work in k1, p1 rib for 12 rounds. Cast off evenly in rib. Press seams.

Child's Sweater

Note: Refer to version you are knitting for colors required.

BACK

Using 3.75mm needles, cast on 104 (112) sts. Work in k1, p1 rib for 16 rows. Change to 4.00mm needles. Using st st, beg with a k row, foll graph on p. 77 for col changes.* Work 140 rows. Cast off.

BACK & FRONTS

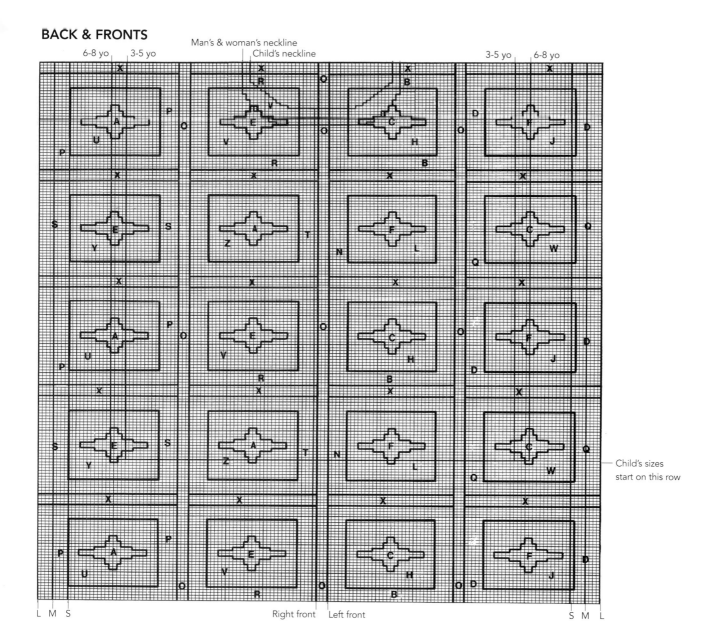

FRONT

Work as given for back to *. Work 124 rows.

Shape front neck Work 43 (47) sts, turn, and leave rem sts on a holder. Work each side of neck separately. Cast off 2 sts at beg of next row and 1 st at neck edge foll rows, 8 times [33 (37) sts]. Work 6 rows. Cast off.
With rs facing, leave 18 sts on a holder, rejoin yarn to rem sts and complete second side to match first side, rev all shaping.

SLEEVES

Using 3.75 mm needles, cast on 38 (42) sts. Work in k1, p1 rib for 15 rows, ending with a rs row.

Next row (inc) Rib 4 (6), m1, [rib 5 (5), m1] 6 times, rib 4 (6) [45 (49) sts].

Change to 4.00mm needles. Using st st, beg with a k row, foll graph on p. 76 for col changes. AT THE SAME TIME, shape sides by inc 1 st at each end of 7 (7)th row and foll 4 (4)th rows, 16 (19) times [79 (89) sts]. Work 3 (3) rows [73 (86) rows]. Cast off loosely and evenly.

MAKING UP

Work as for adult's sweater "making up" to **.

Neckband Using a 3.75mm circular needle, with rs facing, pick up and k 20 sts down left side front neck; 18 sts from stitch holder across front neck; 20 sts up right side front neck; and 38 sts across back of neck [96 sts]. Work in k1, p1 rib for 11 rounds. Cast off evenly in rib. Press seams.

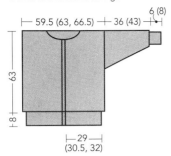

Man's sweater,
woman's and man's cardigan

59.5 (63, 66.5) — 36 (43) — 6 (8)

63

8

29
(30.5, 32)

Woman's and Man's Cardigan

Note: Refer to version you are knitting for colors required.

BACK
Work as for man's sweater back.

LEFT FRONT
Using 3.75mm needles, cast on 65 (69, 73) sts. Work in k1, p1 rib for 26 rows.
Change to 4.00mm needles. Using st st, beg with a k row, foll graph on p. 77 for col changes. Work 168 rows.

Shape front neck Work 55 (59, 63) sts, turn, and leave rem 10 sts on a st holder. Cast off 2 sts at beg of next row and foll alt rows, twice, and 1 st at neck edge of foll alt rows, 3 times [46 (50, 54) sts]. Work 10 rows. Cast off.

RIGHT FRONT
Work as for left front, rev all shaping and foll right front graph on p. 77 for col changes.

SLEEVES
Work as for man's sweater sleeve.

MAKING UP
Work as for man's sweater "making up" to **.

Neckband No. 1 With rs facing and using a 3.75mm circular needle, pick up and k 10 sts from st holder and 28 sts up right front; 44 sts across back neck; 28 sts down left front; and 10 sts from st holder at left front [120 sts]. * Work in k1, p1 rib for 8 rows. Cast off evenly in rib.

Neckband No. 2 Work as for neckband No. 1 to *. Work in k1, p1 rib for 28 rows. Cast off evenly in rib.

Button band With rs facing and using a 3.75mm circular needle, pick up and k 160 sts evenly along front from bottom edge to cast off edge of neckband No 1. or to 8 rows up neckband No. 2. Work in k1, p1 rib for 8 rows. Cast off evenly in rib. Mark position on button band for 6 buttons, the first to come 2cm up from lower edge, the last to come 2cm from top edge, and the remainder spaced evenly between. Sew on buttons.

Buttonhole band Work as for button band, making buttonholes to correspond with position of buttons. Press seams.

Child's Cardigan

Note: Refer to version you are knitting for colors required.

BACK
Work as for child's sweater back.

LEFT FRONT
Using 3.75mm needles, cast on 50 (54) sts. Work in k1, p1 rib for 16 rows.
Change to 4.00mm needles. Using st st, beg with a k row, foll graph on p. 77 for col changes. Work 124 rows.

Shape front neck Work 43 (47) sts, turn, and leave rem 7 sts on a st holder.
Cast off 2 sts at beg of next row and dec 1 st at neck edge on foll rows, 8 times [33 (37) sts]. Work 6 rows [140 (140) rows]. Cast off.

RIGHT FRONT
Work as for left front, rev all shaping and foll right front graph on p. 77 for col changes.

SLEEVES
Work as for child's sweater sleeve.

MAKING UP
Work as for man's sweater "making up" to **.

Neckband With rs facing and using a 3.75mm circular needle, pick up and k 7 sts from st holder and 20 sts up right front; 38 sts across back neck; 20 sts down left front; and 7 sts from st holder at left front [92 sts]. Work in k1, p1 rib for 8 rows. Cast off evenly in rib.

Button band With rs facing and using a 3.75mm circular needle, pick up and k 118 sts evenly along front from bottom edge to cast off edge of neckband. Work in k1, p1 rib for 8 rows. Cast off evenly in rib. Mark position on button band for 4 or 5 buttons, the first to come 1cm up from lower edge, the last to come 1cm down from top edge, and the remainder spaced evenly between. Sew on buttons.

Buttonhole band Work as for button band, making buttonholes to correspond with position of buttons. Press seams.

Version 1—Woman's Cardigan

(Shown in upper left and lower right photos on p. 75.)
Follow basic pattern for woman's and man's cardigan using neckband No. 1 and color sequence for bands as follows:

Fronts and back base bands Cast on col 2, * 2 rows col 2, 2 rows col 1, 2 rows col 3, rep from * 3 times, 2 rows col 2 (26 rows).

Cuffs Cast on col 2, * 2 rows col 2, 2 rows col 1, 2 rows col 3, rep from * 2 times, 2 rows col 2 (20 rows).

Button bands and neckband Pick up sts using col 2, 2 rows col 2, 2 rows col 3, 2 rows col 1, 2 rows col 2 (8 rows). Cast off col 2.

Version 2—Child's Cardigan

(Shown in upper left photo on p. 75.)
Follow basic pattern for child's cardigan using color sequence for bands as follows:

Fronts and back base bands Cast on col 1, 4 rows col 1, 3 rows col 2, 3 rows col 4, 3 rows col 1, 3 rows col 2 (16 rows).

Cuffs Cast on col 1, 5 rows col 1, 3 rows col 4, 3 rows col 2, 5 rows col 1 (16 rows).

Button bands and neckband Pick up sts using col 1, 2 rows col 1, 3 rows col 2, 3 rows col 1 (8 rows). Cast off col 1.

Version 3—Man's Cardigan

(Shown in upper left and lower right photos on p. 75.)
Follow basic pattern for woman's and man's cardigan using neckband No. 2 and color sequence for bands as follows:

Fronts and back base bands Use col 1 throughout.

Cuffs Cast on col 1, 3 rows col 1, 3 rows col 2, 20 rows col 1 (26 rows).

Button bands Use col 1 throughout.

Neckband Foll patt for neckband No. 2 and use col 1 throughout.

Version 4—Child's Sweater

(Shown in upper right photo on p. 75 and in photo at right.)
Follow basic pattern for child's sweater using color sequence for bands as follows:

Front and back base bands Cast on col 1, 4 rows col 1, 4 rows col 2, 4 rows col 4, 4 rows col 3 (16 rows).

Cuffs Cast on col 1, 4 rows col 1, 4 rows col 2, 4 rows col 4, 4 rows col 3 (16 rows).

Neckband Pick up sts using col 3, 3 rows col 3, 3 rows col 4, 3 rows col 2, 2 rows col 1 (11 rows). Cast off col 1.

Version 5—Man's Sweater

(Shown in upper right photo on p. 75.)
Follow basic pattern for man's sweater using neckband No. 1.
Note: When following graph for color changes on front, knit the two small, central-shaped motifs coded C and E either side of the front neck shaping using col 3.
Use color sequence for bands as follows:

Front and back base bands Cast on col 1, 2 rows col 1, 2 rows col 3, 2 rows col 4, 2 rows col 2, 2 rows col 4, 2 rows col 3, 14 rows col 1 (26 rows).

Cuffs Cast on col 1, 2 rows col 1, 2 rows col 2, 2 rows col 3, 20 rows col 1 (26 rows).

Neckband Use col 3 throughout.

Version 6—Child's Cardigan

(Shown in lower left photo on p. 75.)
Follow basic pattern for child's cardigan using color sequence for bands as follows:

Fronts and back base bands Cast on col 4, 3 rows col 4, 2 rows col 3, 2 rows col 2, 2 rows col 3, 7 rows col 1 (16 rows).

Cuffs Cast on col 4, 3 rows col 4, 2 rows col 3, 2 rows col 2, 2 rows col 3, 7 rows col 1 (16 rows).

Button bands and neckband Pick up sts using col 3. Work 2 rows col 3, 2 rows col 2, 2 rows col 3, 2 rows col 4 (8 rows). Cast off col 4.

Version 7—Woman's Cardigan

(Shown in lower left photo on p. 75.)
Follow basic pattern for woman's and man's cardigan using neckband No. 1 and color sequence for bands as follows:

Fronts and back base bands Cast on col 1, 3 rows col 1, 3 rows col 3, 3 rows col 5, 17 rows col 1 (26 rows).

Cuffs Cast on col 1, 3 rows col 1, 3 rows col 3, 3 rows col 5, 11 rows col 1 (20 rows).

Button bands and neckband Use col 1 throughout (8 rows).

Child's sweater, cardigan

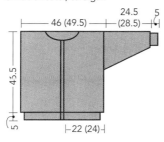

MONET

WOMAN'S SWEATER

This pattern is suitable for an experienced knitter with knowledge of intarsia knitting (see instructions on pp. 7-8). This is a loose-fitting, drop-shouldered sweater in one size only.

NEEDLES
- 1 pair 3.25mm (USA 3) (UK 10)
- 1 pair 4.00mm (USA 6) (UK 8)
- 3.25mm circular needle 60cm (USA 3) (UK 10)

TENSION
22.5 sts and 30 rows to 10cm, measured over patterned stockinette stitch using 4.00mm needles.

YARN
Jo Sharp 8-ply DK Pure-Wool Handknitting Yarn

Key		Color	Quantity	
1		Terracotta 332	7	x 50g
2	c	Naples 321	2	x 50g
3	⊠	Brick 333	1	x 50g
4	☑	Mulberry 325	1	x 50g
5	⊿	Slate 328	3	x 50g
6	c	Chartreuse 330	2	x 50g
7	⊠	Avocado 337	2	x 50g
8	☑	Daisy 315	3	x 50g
9	⊿	Violet 319	3	x 50g
10	·	Gold 320	2	x 50g

BACK
Using 3.25mm needles and col 1, cast on 134 sts. Work 22 rows of k1, p1 rib. Change to 4.00mm needles. Using st st and beg with a k row, foll graph on p. 82 for col changes (see note on graph).* Work 204 rows.

Shape shoulders Cast off 9 sts at the beg of next 10 rows (44 sts). Leave rem 44 sts on a holder.

FRONT
Work as given for back to *. Work 178 rows.

Shape front neck Patt 55 sts, turn, and leave rem sts on a holder. Work each side of neck separately. Cast off 1 st at neck edge on next 6 rows and 1 st on foll alt rows 4 times (45 sts). Patt 11 rows.

Shape shoulders Cast off 9 sts at beg of next and foll alt rows 5 times. With rs facing, leave 24 sts on a holder, rejoin yarn to rem sts, and complete second side to match first side, rev all shaping.

SLEEVES
(Note two different sleeve designs.)
Using 3.25mm needles and col 1, cast on 56 sts. Work 21 rows in k1, p1 rib.

Next row (inc) Rib 1, (m1, rib 3) 18 times, m1, rib 1 (75 sts). Change to 4.00mm needles. Using st st and beg with a k row, foll graphs on p. 83 for col changes. AT THE SAME TIME, shape sides by inc 1 st at each end of 5th row and every foll 4th row 18 times, and foll 6th row 6 times (125 sts). Take extra sts into patt as they occur. Work 7 rows (120 rows). Cast off loosely and evenly.

*Note: When working from
graphs for the front and two
sleeves, read odd rows (k)
from right to left and even rows
(p) from left to right. Read the
back graph in reverse; that is,
read odd rows (k) from left to
right and even rows (p) from
right to left.*

FRONT & BACK

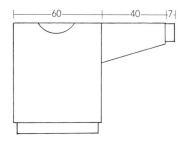

MAKING UP

Press all pieces, except ribbing, gently on ws
using a warm iron over a damp cloth. Using
backstitch, join shoulder seams.

Collar With rs facing and using 3.25mm circular
needle and col 9, beg at center front, pick up
and k 12 sts from st holder; 42 sts up right side
front neck; 44 sts from st holder across back of
neck; 42 sts down left side front neck; and the
rem 12 sts on holder at front neck
(152 sts). Work 2.5cm in k1, p1 rib, working in
rounds and finishing at center front.

Divide for collar

Now, working backward and forward in rows,
turning at center front, cont in rib until collar
measures 9cm from pick-up row. Cast off evenly
in rib. Center sleeves and join. Join side and
sleeve seams, using edge-to-edge stitch on ribs.
Press seams.

LEFT
SLEEVE

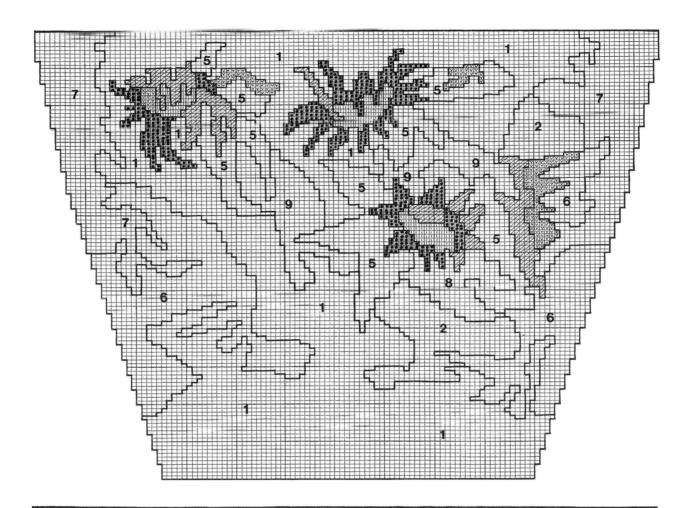

RIGHT
SLEEVE

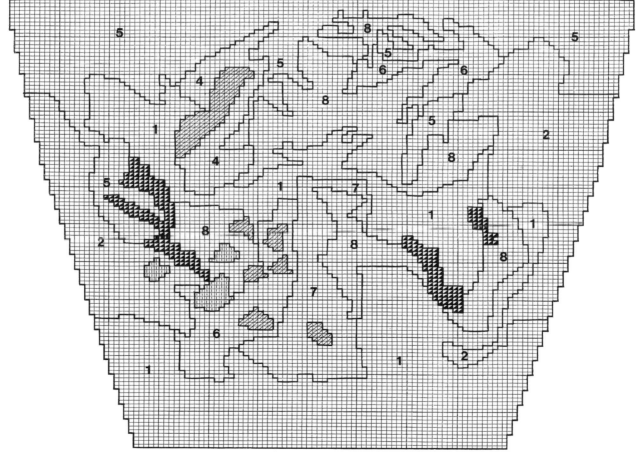

PALMS & CAMOMILE

WOMAN'S CARDIGAN

The Palms and Camomile designs are suitable for an average-skilled knitter with knowledge of intarsia knitting (see instructions on pp. 7–8). Version 1: Cardigan with moss stitch cuffs, collar, and button bands. Broad moss stitch borders incorporate pockets. The skirt is shaped with an elastic waistband. Version 2: Cardigan with a knitted lace border and a crocheted edge around front, neck, and cuffs.

NEEDLES
- I pair 4.00mm (USA 6) (UK 8)
- Version I—I pair 3.25mm (USA 3) (UK I0)
- Skirt—I pair 5.00mm (USA 8) (UK 6)
- Version 2—3.50mm crochet hook (USA E/4) (UK 9)

BUTTONS
Version I—Eight 2cm
Version 2—Five Icm

TENSION
22.5 sts and 30 rows to 10cm, measured over patterned stockinette stitch using 4.00mm needles.

YARN
Jo Sharp 8-ply DK Pure-Wool Handknitting Yarn

Key	Color	Quantity			
		S	(M	L)	
VERSION 1					
1	Forest 318	8	8	9	x 50g
2	Jade 316	5	5	5	x 50g
3	Lilac 324	5	5	5	x 50g
4	Smoke 339	11	12	12	x 50g
5	Wedgewood 340	2	2	2	x 50g
6	Ginger 322	1	1	1	x 50g
VERSION 2					
1	Gold 320	4	5	5	x 50g
2	Coral 304	4	5	5	x 50g
3	Cherry 309	5	5	5	x 50g
4	Wine 307	6	6	6	x 50g
5	Lobelia 306	2	2	2	x 50g
6	Leaf 310	1	1	1	x 50g

Version 1

BACK
Using 3.25mm needles and col 1, cast on 124 (132, 140) sts. Work band in moss st (i.e., work in k1, p1 across first row, then in subsequent rows, k all the p sts and p all the k sts, as they face you) for 64 rows. Change to 4.00mm needles. Using st st beg with a k row, foll graph on p. 86 for col changes. Patt 164 rows.

Shape shoulders Cast off 9 (10, 11) sts at beg of next 8 rows and 11 (11, 11) sts at beg of foll 2 rows. Leave rem 30 sts on a st holder.

POCKET LININGS (MAKE 2)
Using 3.25mm needles and col 1, cast on 50 sts. Using moss st, work 56 rows. Leave sts on a st holder.

LEFT FRONT
Using 3.25mm needles and col 1, cast on 62 (66, 70) sts. Work in moss st for 60 rows*.

Row 61—Place pocket linings Moss st 6 (10, 14) sts, sl next 50 sts onto a st holder, and in place of these, moss st across 50 sts of first pocket lining, moss st 6 (6, 6). Cont in moss st for another 3 rows (64 rows). Change to 4.00mm needles. Using st st beg with a k row, foll graph on p. 86 for col changes. Patt 144 rows.

Shape front neck Patt 54 (58, 62) sts, turn, and leave rem 8 sts on a st holder. Cast off 1 st at beg of next and foll alt rows 7 times [47 (51, 55) sts]. Patt 6 rows.

Shape shoulders Cast off 9 (10, 11) sts at beg of next and foll alt rows 4 times. Patt 1 row. Cast off rem 11 sts.

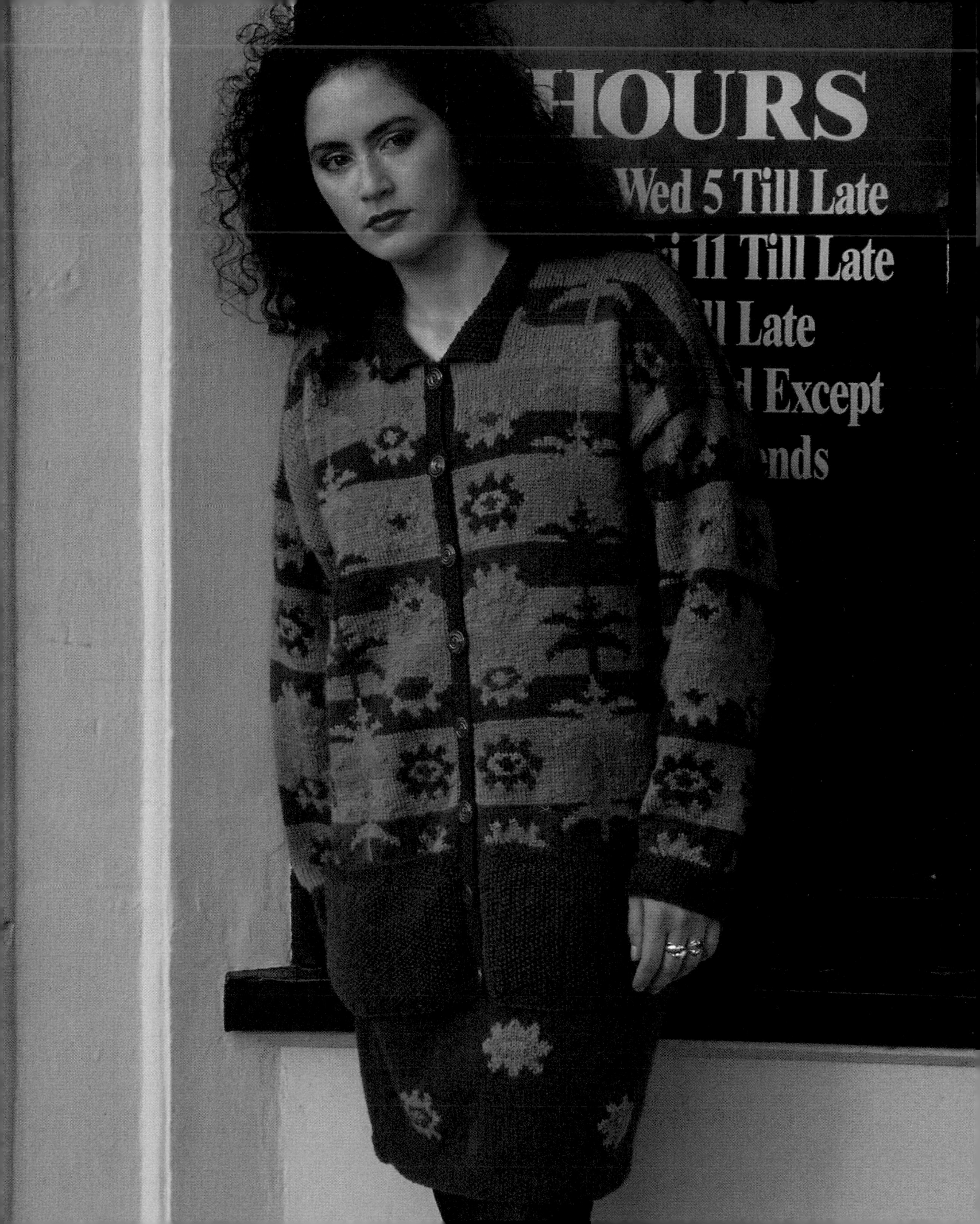
HOURS
Wed 5 Till Late
11 Till Late
Late
Except

FRONTS, BACK & SLEEVES

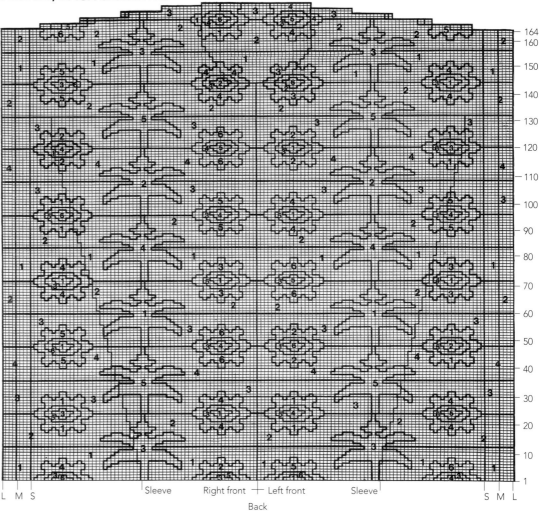

L M S ... Sleeve ... Right front — Left front ... Sleeve ... S M L

Back

164 · 160 · 150 · 140 · 130 · 120 · 110 · 100 · 90 · 80 · 70 · 60 · 50 · 40 · 30 · 20 · 10 · 1

RIGHT FRONT
Work as for left front to *.

Row 61—Place pocket lining Moss st 6 (6, 6), sl next 50 sts onto a st holder, and in place of these, moss st across 50 sts of second pocket lining, moss st 6 (10, 14). Cont in moss st for another 3 rows (64 rows). Cont as for left front, rev all shaping and foll graph above for right front col changes.

SLEEVES
Using 3.25mm needles and col 4, cast on 54 sts. Work 4 rows in moss st. Change to col 1, and work a further 14 rows in moss st (18 rows) inc in last row to 66 sts. Change to 4.00mm needles. Using st st beg with a k row, foll graph above for col changes. AT THE SAME TIME, shape sides by inc 1 st at each end of 7th row and foll 6th row 23 times (114 sts), taking extra sts into patt as they occur. Patt 10 rows (132 rows). Cast off loosely and evenly.

SKIRT (MAKE 2)
Using 3.25mm needles and col 4, cast on 99 (105, 111) sts. Work 10 rows in moss st. Change to 4.00mm needles. Using st st beg with a k row, foll graph on p. 87 for col changes. AT THE SAME TIME, shape sides by inc 1 st at each end of 7th and foll 8th rows 3 times, then inc 1 st at each end of foll 10th rows 3 times [111 (117, 123) sts]. Cont without further shaping for 77 rows (140 rows) or until length desired.

Next 2 rows Change to 5.00mm needles. *(This forms fold line for waistband.)* Change back to 4.00mm needles, and cont in st st for 8 rows. Cast off.

MAKING UP
Press all pieces gently on ws using a warm iron over a damp cloth. Using backstitch, join shoulder seams. Center sleeves into armholes

SKIRT

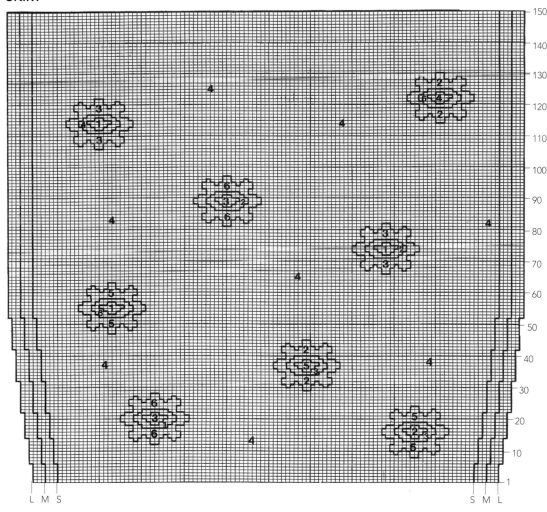

and join. Join side and sleeve seams using edge-to-edge stitch on bands.

Button band Using 3.25mm needles and col 4, cast on 6 sts. Work in moss st until the band is long enough when slightly stretched to fit along front edge of cardigan. Mark position on button band for 8 buttons, the first to come 1.5cm up from lower edge, the last to come 1.5cm down from top edge, and the remainder spaced evenly between.

Buttonhole band Work as for button band, making buttonholes to correspond with position of buttons. Pin and sew bands into place. AT THE SAME TIME, cast off the 3 outer-edge sts and slip the rem 3 sts onto the holder at front neck (11 sts). Sew on buttons to correspond with buttonholes.

Collar With rs facing and using col 1 and 3.25mm needles, pick up the 11 sts off holder at right front; then 25 sts up right front neck; 30 sts from holder at back neck; 25 sts down left front neck; and 11 sts off rem holder (102 sts). Work 7 rows in moss st.

Next row Change to 4.00mm needles, and cont in moss st for 12 rows. Change to col 4, and work 5 rows in moss st. Cast off.

Pocket tops Using 3.25mm needles and col 4, work 6 rows moss st across sts left on st holder. Cast off evenly. Sew pocket linings into place on ws, and finish off pocket tops on rs.

Skirt Using backstitch, join side seams using edge-to-edge st on moss st. Fold waistband over and sl st. Insert elastic. Press seams.

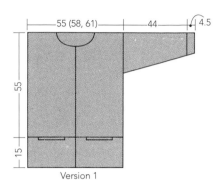

55 (58, 61)   44   4.5

55

15

Version 1

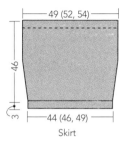

49 (52, 54)

46

3

44 (46, 49)

Skirt

Version 2

BACK
Using 4.00mm needles and col 1, cast on 124 (132, 140) sts. Working in st st beg with a k row, foll graph on p. 86 for col changes. Patt 164 rows.

Shape shoulders Cast off 9 (10, 11) sts at beg of next 8 rows, and 11 (11, 11) sts at beg of foll 2 rows. Cast off rem 30 sts.

LEFT FRONT
Using 4.00mm needles and col 1, cast on 62 (66, 70) sts. Working in st st beg with a k row, foll graph on p. 86 for col changes. Patt 144 rows.

Shape front neck Patt 54 (58, 62) sts, turn, and leave rem 8 sts on a holder. Cast off 1 st on next and foll alt rows 7 times [47 (51, 55) sts]. Patt 6 rows.

Shape shoulders Cast off 9 (10, 11) sts at beg of next and foll alt rows 4 times. Patt 1 row. Cast off rem 11 sts.

RIGHT FRONT
Work as for left front, rev all shaping, and foll graph on p. 86 for right front col changes.

SLEEVES
Using 4.00mm needles and col 1, cast on 66 sts. Working in st st beg with a k row, foll graph on p. 86 for col changes. AT THE SAME TIME, shape sides by inc 1 st at each end of 7th row and every foll 6th row 23 times (114 sts), taking extra sts into patt as they occur. Patt 10 rows (132 rows). Cast off loosely and evenly.

MAKING UP

Press all pieces gently on ws using a warm iron over a damp cloth. Using backstitch, join shoulder seams. Center sleeves into armholes and join. Join side and sleeve seams.

Lace border Using 4.00mm needles and col 4, cast on 8 sts.

1st foundation row On rs, k6, k into front and back of next st, yf, sl1 purlwise (9 sts).

2nd foundation row Kb1, k1, [yf, sl1, k1, psso, k1] twice, yf, sl1 purlwise (9 sts).

Row 1 Kb1, k to last st, k into front and back of last st, turn, and cast on 2 sts (12 sts).

Row 2 K1, k into front and back of next st, k2, [yf, sl1, k1, psso, k1] twice, yf, k1, yf, sl1 purlwise (14 sts).

Row 3 Kb1, k to last 2 sts, k into front and back of next st, yf, sl1 purlwise (15 sts).

Row 4 Kb1, k into front and back of next st, k2, [yf, sl1, k1, psso, k1] 3 times, k1, yf, sl1 purlwise (16 sts).

Row 5 Kb1, k to last 2 sts, k2 tog (15 sts).

Row 6 Sl1 purlwise, k1, psso, sl1, k1, psso, k4, [yf, sl1, k1, psso, k1] twice, yf, sl1 purlwise (13 sts).

Row 7 Kb1, k to last 2 sts, k2tog (12 sts).

Row 8 Cast off 3 sts (1 st on right-hand needle), k2, yf, sl1, k1, psso, k1, yf, sl1, k1, psso, yf, sl1 purlwise (9 sts).
Rep these 8 rows until lace border is long enough to fit around bottom of cardigan,

ending on an 8th row. Cast off. With rs facing, pin lace border to bottom of cardigan and sl st into position.

Crochet front and neck edging With rs facing and using a 3.50mm crochet hook and col 4, join yarn with a sl st to bottom edge of lace border on right front. Work 3ch, 3tr in same spot, *miss approx 1cm, 1 dc, miss approx 1cm, 4tr in same spot. Rep from * up right front edge, around back of neck, and down left front edge, spacing sts so that edging lies flat and there are the same number of treble clusters on each side.

Buttons Sew buttons to center of treble clusters on left front. Place first button at start of neck shaping, last button where lace border joins body, and the remaining 3 spaced evenly between. Each button fastens through the center of a treble cluster on right front.

Crochet cuff edging Work as given for front and neck edging. Press seams.

```
|———55 (58, 61)———|——44——|↑ 1
```

Version 2

PRIMITIVE BIRD

WOMAN'S SWEATER

The Primitive Bird sweater is drop shouldered and loose fitting. This pattern is easy to follow and is suitable for an average knitter with knowledge of intarsia knitting (see instructions on pp. 7–8).

NEEDLES

- I pair 3.25mm (USA 3) (UK 10)
- I pair 4.00mm (USA 6) (UK 8)
- 3.25mm circular needle (USA 3) (UK 10) or a set of double-pointed needles

TENSION

22.5 sts and 30 rows to 10cm, measured over patterned stockinette stitch using 4.00mm needles.

YARN

Jo Sharp 8-ply DK Pure-Wool Handknitting Yarn

Key	Color		Quantity			
	VERSION 1	**VERSION 2**	**S**	**(M**	**L)**	
1	Slate 328	Antique 323	12	12	13	x 50g
2	Gold 320	Gold 320	1	1	1	x 50g
3	Khaki 329	Smoke 339	1	1	1	x 50g
4	Olive 313	Ginger 322	2	2	2	x 50g
5	Brick 333	Lilac 324	2	2	2	x 50g
6	Lilac 324	Earth 334	2	2	2	x 50g
7	Violet 319	Olive 313	1	1	1	x 50g
8	Jade 316	Violet 319	1	1	1	x 50g

BACK

Using 3.25mm needles and col 1, cast on 128 (134, 140) sts. Work in pique rib as follows:

Row 1 On rs, k4 (2, 0), *p3, k1, p3, k3. Rep from * to last 4 (2, 0) sts, p4 (2, 0).

Row 2 K4 (2, 0), *p3, k3, p1, k3. Rep from * to last 4 (2, 0) sts, p4 (2, 0).

Row 3 Follow directions for row 1.

Row 4 Knit.
Rep rows 1 to 4, 4 times, and then rows 1 and 2 once (22 rows). Change to 4.00mm needles. Using st st beg with a k row, foll graph on p. 92 for col changes. **Work 182 (190, 198) rows. Cast off 42 (45, 48) sts at beg of next two rows. Leave rem 44 sts on a holder.

FRONT

Work as given for back to **. Work 158 (166, 174) rows.

Shape front neck Patt 52 (55, 58) sts, turn, and leave rem sts on a holder. Work each side of neck separately. Cast off 2 sts at neck edge on foll alt rows 3 times, and 1 st on foll alt rows 4 times [42 (45, 48) sts]. Patt 10 rows. Cast off. With rs facing, leave 24 sts on a holder. Rejoin yarn to rem sts, and complete second side to match first side, rev all shaping.

SLEEVES

Using 3.25mm needles and col 1, cast on 60 sts and work in pique rib as follows:

Row 1 On rs, *p3, k1, p3, k3, rep from * to end.

Row 2 *P3, k3, p1, k3, rep from * to end.

Row 3 Follow directions for row 1.

Version 1 shown at right.

FRONT & BACK

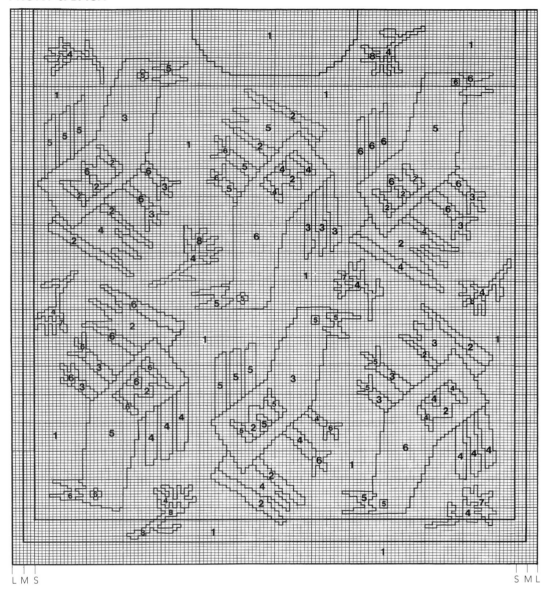

L M S   S M L

Row 4 Knit.
Rep rows 1 to 4, 4 times, then rows 1 and 2 once, increasing to 75 sts on the last row. Change to 4.00mm needles. Using st st beg with a k row, foll graph on p. 93 for col changes. AT THE SAME TIME, shape sides by inc 1 st at each end of 7th row and every foll 6th row 6 times, and every foll 4th row 17 times (123 sts). Work 3 rows (114 rows) or until length desired. Cast off loosely and evenly.

MAKING UP
Press all pieces, except ribbing, gently on ws using a warm iron over a damp cloth. Using backstitch, join shoulder seams. Center sleeves and join. Join side and sleeve seams using edge-to-edge stitch on ribs.

Neckband Using a 3.25mm circular needle and col 1, with rs facing, pick up and k 31 sts down left side front neck; 24 st from holder at center front; 31 sts up right side front neck; and 44 sts from holder at back neck (130 sts).

Round 1 *P3, k1, p3, k3, rep from * to end.

Round 2 Follow directions for round 1.

Round 3 Follow directions for round 1.

Round 4 Purl.
Repeat these 4 rounds 3 times. Cast off loosely and evenly.

SLEEVE

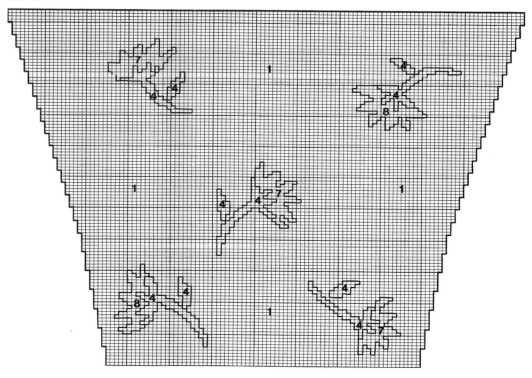

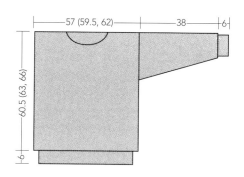

Version 2 shown at left.

ROMANTIC

WOMAN'S SWEATER

The Romantic sweater is drop shouldered with a split polo collar and simple embroidered motifs. This pattern is suitable for a beginner knitter who has basic needlework skills.

NEEDLES
• I pair 3.25mm (USA 3) (UK 10)
• I pair 4.00mm (USA 6) (UK 8)
• 3.25mm circular needle (USA 3) (UK 10) or set of 4 double-pointed needles
• Embroidery needle

TENSION
22.5 sts and 30 rows to 10cm, measured over stockinette stitch using 4.00mm needles.

YARN
Jo Sharp 8-ply DK Pure-Wool Handknitting Yarn

Key	Color	Quantity			
		S	(M	L)	
1	Lilac 324	12	12	13	x 50g
2	Smoke 339	4	4	4	x 50g
	Brick 333	1	1	1	x 50g
	Gold 320	1	1	1	x 50g
	Antique 323	1	1	1	x 50g
	Terracotta 332	1	1	1	x 50g

BACK
Using 3.25mm needles and col 2, cast on 132 (138, 144) sts. Work 12cm in k2, p2 rib, ending with a ws row. Change to 4.00mm needles, and work in st st for 20 rows. Change to col 1 and cont in st st for a further 82 (88, 94) rows.

Shape armholes Cast off 10 sts at beg of next 2 rows [112 (118, 124) sts].* Work a further 66 rows in st st.

Shape shoulders Cast off 8 (9, 10) sts at beg of next 8 rows and 9 (8, 7) sts at beg of foll 2 rows. Leave rem 30 sts on a holder.

FRONT
Work as given for back to *. Work a further 52 rows.

Shape front neck Work 48 (51, 54) sts, turn, and leave rem sts on a holder. Work each side of neck separately. Cast off 1 st at neck edge on next 4 rows and 1 st on foll alt rows 3 times. Work 3 rows.

Shape shoulders Cast off 8 (9, 10) sts at beg of next and alt rows 4 times. Work 1 row. Cast off rem 9 (8, 7) sts. With rs facing, leave 16 sts on a holder. Rejoin yarn to rem sts, and complete second side to match first side, rev all shaping.

SLEEVES
Using 3.25mm needles and col 2, cast on 56 sts. Work 4 rows in k2, p2 rib. Change to col 1 and cont in k2, p2 rib until cuff measures 14cm, ending with a rs row.

Next row (inc) Rib 4, (m1, rib 6) 8 times, m1, rib 4 (65 sts).
Change to 4.00mm needles, and cont using st st, beg with a k row. AT THE SAME TIME, shape sides by inc 1 st at each end of 7th row and every foll 6th row 6 times, then every foll 4th row 13 times (105 sts). Cont without further shaping until work measures 50cm or length desired. Cast off loosely and evenly.

MAKING UP
Press all pieces, except ribbing, gently on ws, using a warm iron over a damp cloth. Using backstitch, join shoulder seams. Center sleeves and join. Embroider following diagram and instructions on p. 97, using an embroidery needle and colors as set.

Collar With rs facing and using a 3.25mm circular needle and col 1, beg at center front, pick up and k 8 sts from st holder, 27 sts up right side front neck; 30 sts from st holder across back

of neck; 27 sts down left side front neck; and the rem 8 sts on holder at front neck (100 sts). Work 16 rows in k2, p2 rib, turning at center front. Change to col 2, and cont in k2, p2 rib for a further 4 rows. Cast off evenly in rib. Join side and sleeve seams using edge-to-edge stitch on ribs. Press seams.

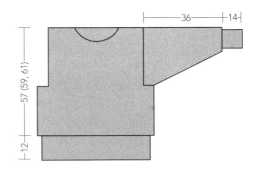

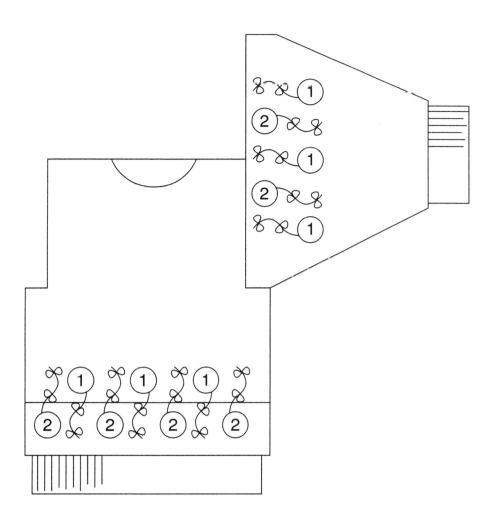

EMBROIDERY INSTRUCTIONS

Use split yarn throughout. (Yarn is made up of four strands. Divide these into two groups of two, and pull apart to make the finer yarn used for embroidery.)

Daisy flowers	No. 1	No. 2
Central lazy daisy	Smoke 339	Antique 323
Spikes around central lazy daisy	Brick 333	Gold 320
French knot in center	Antique 323	Lilac 324
Inner circle	Terracotta 332	Brick 333
Outer circle	Gold 320	Terracotta 332

Stems and leaves

Stem stitch stems and lazy daisy stitch leaves, using smoke on lilac background and lilac on smoke background.

RUSTIC TEXTURE

WOMAN'S SWEATER AND CARDIGAN

The Rustic Texture sweater and cardigan are drop shouldered with a V neckline. This pattern features a simple texture and is suitable for a beginner knitter.

NEEDLES
- I pair 3.25mm (USA 3) (UK I0)
- I pair 4.00mm (USA 6) (UK 8)
- 3.25mm circular needle (USA 3) (UK I0)

BUTTONS
Woman's cardigan—Seven I.5cm

TENSION
25 sts and 30 rows to I0cm, measured over supple rib pattern using 4.00mm needles.

SUPPLE RIB PATTERN
Multiple of 3 + I
Row I On rs, kI, *k the next st but do not slip it off the left-hand needle, then p the same st and the next st tog, kI, rep from * to end.
Row 2 Purl.
Rep these 2 rows.

YARN
Jo Sharp 8-ply DK Pure-Wool Handknitting Yarn

	Color	Quantity			
		S	(M	L)	
Woman's Sweater	Ruby 326	16	16	17	x 50g
Woman's Cardigan	Linen 335	16	16	17	x 50g

Woman's Sweater

BACK
Using 3.25mm needles, cast on 139 (145, 151) sts and k 3 rows. Change to 4.00mm needles, and cont in supple rib patt for* 184 (194, 204) rows. Cast off.

FRONT
Work as given for back to *. Work 132 (142, 152) rows.

Shape front neck Patt 69 (72, 75) sts, turn, and leave rem sts on a holder. Work each side of neck separately. Keeping supple rib patt correct, dec 1 st at neck edge on next and foll alt rows 10 times [59 (62, 66) sts], then every 4th row 7 times [52 (55, 58) sts]. Patt 4 rows [184 (194, 204) rows]. Cast off. With rs facing, rejoin yarn to rem sts. Cast off center st, and patt to end. Complete second side to match first side, rev all shaping.

SLEEVES
Using 3.25mm needles, cast on 55 sts and k 3 rows. Change to 4.00mm needles, and cont in supple rib patt. AT THE SAME TIME, shape sides by inc 1 st at each end of 5th and foll 4th rows 29 times [113 sts]. Patt 3 rows [120 rows] or until length desired. Cast off loosely and evenly.

MAKING UP
Press all pieces gently on ws using a warm iron over a damp cloth. Using backstitch, join shoulder seams. Center sleeves and join. Join side and sleeve seams. ** Press seams.

Woman's sweater

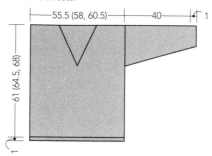

Woman's Cardigan

BACK
Work as for sweater back.

POCKET LININGS (MAKE 2)
Using 4.00mm needles, cast on 36 sts. Work 42 rows in st st, beg with a k row. Leave sts on a holder.

LEFT FRONT
Using 3.25mm needles, cast on 70 (73, 76) sts and k 3 rows. Change to 4.00mm needles, and cont in supple rib patt for 42 rows*.

Row 43—Place pocket lining Patt 16 (19, 22) sts, slip next 36 sts on a holder, and in place of these, patt across 36 sts of first pocket lining, patt 18 (18, 18) sts. Cont in patt until 131 (141, 151) patt rows completed.

Shape front neck edge Keeping supple rib patt correct, dec 1 st at neck edge on next and foll alt rows 11 times, then 1 st every 4th row 7 times [52 (55, 58) sts]. Patt 3 rows [184 (194, 204) rows]. Cast off.

SLEEVES
Work as for sweater sleeve.

MAKING UP
Work as for sweater "making up" until **.

Front band (worked in one piece) With rs facing and using 3.25mm circular needle, pick up 88 (94, 100) sts on right front from cast-on edge to beg of neck shaping; 44 sts to shoulder seam; 38 sts across back neck; 44 sts down left front to beg of neck shaping; and 88 (94, 100) sts down to cast-on edge.

Row 1 Knit.

Row 2—Place buttonholes K3, cast off 2 sts, *k11 (12, 13), cast off 2 sts, rep from * 5 times, k to end.

Row 3 Knit, casting on 2 sts over those cast off on previous row. Cast off evenly. Sew on buttons to correspond with buttonholes.

Pocket tops With rs facing and 3.25mm needles, k 3 rows across stitches left on holder. Cast off evenly. Sew pocket linings into place on ws, and finish off pocket tops on rs. Press seams.

Woman's cardigan

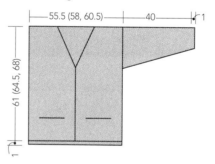

CABLE AND MOSS

WOMAN'S CARDIGAN, MAN'S AND CHILD'S SWEATER

This pattern is suitable for an average-skilled knitter and uses a slip stitch to create a cable effect. All garments are loose fitting and drop shouldered.

NEEDLES
- I pair 3.25mm (USA 3) (UK IO)
- I pair 4.00mm (USA 6) (UK 8)
- I pair 5.00mm (USA 8) (UK 6)

BUTTONS
Woman's cardigan—Five 2cm

TENSION
2I sts and 30 rows to IOcm, measured over cable and moss pattern using 5.00mm needles.

SPECIAL ABBREVIATIONS
C3l (cable 3 left) = slip next st onto cable needle and hold at front of work, knit next 2 sts from left-hand needle, then knit st from cable needle.
C3r (cable 3 right) = slip next 2 sts onto cable needle and hold at back of work, knit next st from left-hand needle, then knit sts from cable needle.

STITCH NOTE
Cable pattern worked over 9 sts and 8 rows.
Row I (Rs) kI, slI purlwise, k5, slI purlwise, kI.
Row 2 PI, slI purlwise, p5, slI purlwise, pI.
Row 3 KI, c3l, kI, c3r, kI.
Row 4 Purl.
Row 5 K3, slI purlwise, kI, slI purlwise, k3.
Row 6 P3, slI purlwise, pI, slI purlwise, p3.
Row 7 KI, c3r, kI, c3l, kI.
Row 8 Purl. Repeat these 8 rows.

MOSS STITCH PATTERN
Row I (Rs) kI, *pI, kI, rep from * to end.
Row 2 (Ws) kI, *pI, kI, rep from * to end.

Woman's Cardigan

BACK
Using 4.00mm needles, cast on 141 (145, 149) sts. Work 20 rows in k1, p1 rib, ending with a ws row. Change to 5.00mm needles.

Row 1 Moss st 2 (4, 6) [row 1 cable patt, moss st 7] 8 times, row 1 cable patt, moss st 2 (4, 6). *This row sets the position of patt.* Cont in patt until 194 (204, 214) rows have been completed. Cast off.

POCKET LININGS (MAKE 2)
Using 5.00mm needles, cast on 39 sts. Work 42 rows in st st beg with a k row. Leave sts on a holder.

LEFT FRONT
Using 4.00mm needles, cast on 66 (68, 70) sts. Work 20 rows in k1, p1 rib, ending with a ws row. Change to 5.00mm needles.*

YARN
Jo Sharp 8-ply DK Pure-Wool Handknitting Yarn

	Color	Quantity			
		S	**(M**	**L)**	
Woman's Cardigan	Mulberry 325	18	19	19	x 50g
Man's Sweater	Slate 328	17	18	18	x 50g
		3-5	**(6-8) yo**		
Child's Sweater	Violet 319	9	10		x 50g

Woman's L back/front
Woman's M back/front
Woman's S back/front

Man's L back/front
Man's M back/front
Man's S back/front

Child's 6-8 yo back/front
Child's 3-5 yo back/front

Man's sleeve
Woman's sleeve
Child's sleeve

Right front

Graph continued on p. 105

KEY

☐ K on rs, p on ws
⊡ P on rs, k on ws
← C3l
→ C3r
V Sl st

Row 1 Moss st 2 (4, 6), [row 1 of cable patt, moss st 7] 4 times. *This row sets position of patt.* Cont in patt for 50 rows.

Row 51—Place pocket lining Patt 11 (13, 15). Slip next 39 sts onto a holder, and in place of these, patt across 39 sts of first pocket lining, patt 16 (16, 16). Cont in patt until 125 (135, 145) patt rows completed.

Shape front neck Keeping armhole edge straight, dec 2 sts at neck edge on next row and 1 st on every foll 4th row 16 times, 48 (50, 52) sts. Work 4 rows. Cast off.

RIGHT FRONT

Work as given for left front to *.

Row 1 [Moss st 7, row 1 cable patt] 4 times, moss st 2 (4, 6). *This row sets position of patt.* Cont in patt for 50 rows.

Row 51 Patt 16, slip next 39 sts onto a holder, and in place of these, patt across 39 sts of second pocket lining, patt 11 (13, 15). Cont as given for left front, rev all shaping.

SLEEVES

Using 3.25mm needles, cast on 56 sts. Work 19 rows in k1, p1 rib.

Next row (inc) On ws, rib 4, [m1, rib 6] 8 times, m1, rib 4 (65 sts). Change to 5.00mm needles.

Row 1 Moss st 4, [row 1 cable patt, moss st 7] 3 times, row 1 cable patt, moss st 4. *This row sets position of patt.* Cont in patt. AT THE SAME TIME, shape sides by inc 1 st each end of 5th row and every foll 6th row 16 times (99 sts). Take extra sts into patt as they occur. Patt another 3 rows (104 rows) or until length desired. Cast off.

MAKING UP

Press all pieces, except ribbing, gently on ws using a warm iron over a damp cloth. Using backstitch, join shoulder seams. Center sleeves and join. Join side and sleeve seams using edge-to-edge stitch on ribs.

Front band Using 4.00mm needles, cast on 17 sts.

Row 1 K1, row 1 cable patt, moss st 7. *This row sets position of patt (note the extra k st before the cable patt is worked as a p st on even rows and is used when sewing band into position).* Work in patt until band is long enough when slightly stretched to fit up left front to center back. With rs facing and cable panel of band closest to seam, pin this section of band into place. Mark position of buttons on rs of cable panel, the first to come 2cm up from lower edge, the last to come 2cm down from start of neck shaping, and the remainder to be spaced evenly between. Cont with band to fit down right front when slightly stretched, making buttonholes to correspond with button positions. Note: Because the front band is folded to double thickness, 2 corresponding horizontal buttonholes must be made for each button as follows:

Buttonhole Row (rs) patt 4, cast off 3, patt 5, cast off 3, patt 2.

Next row Work row in patt, casting on 3 sts in place of those cast off in previous row. Sew band into position. Fold band in half (ws together), and sew moss st edge to inside edge of hem. Sew buttonholes together. Sew on buttons to correspond with buttonholes.

Pocket tops Using 4.00mm needles, work 8 rows k1, p1 rib across sts left on holder. Cast off evenly on rib. Sew pocket linings into place on ws and finish pocket tops on rs. Press seams.

Man's Sweater

BACK

Using 5.00mm needles, cast on 127 (131, 135) sts.

Row 1 Moss st 3 (5, 7), [row 1 cable patt, moss st 7] 7 times, row 1 cable patt, moss st 3 (5, 7). *This row sets position of patt.*** Cont in patt until row 194 (204, 214) has been completed (or length desired). Cast off.

Woman's cardigan

67 (69, 71) — 34 — 6
64 (68, 71)
6

Man's sweater

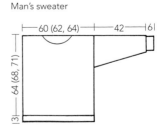

60 (62, 64) — 42 — 6
64 (68, 71)
3

FRONT

Work as given for back to **. Cont in patt for 172 (182, 192) rows.

Next row, shape front neck Patt 58 (60, 62) sts, turn, and leave rem sts on a holder. Work each side of neck separately. Cast off 3 sts at beg of next and foll alt rows 4 times and 1 st on foll alt rows 3 times [43 (45, 47) sts]. Patt 8 rows. Cast off. With rs facing, rejoin yarn to rem sts, cast off center 11 sts, patt to end. Complete to match first side, rev all shaping.

SLEEVES

Using 3.25mm needles, cast on 56 sts. Work 19 rows in k1, p1 rib.

Next row (inc) On ws, rib 1, m1, rib3, m1, [rib 4, m1] 12 times, rib 3, m1, rib 1 (71 sts). Change to 5.00mm needles.

Row 1 [Moss st 7, row 1 cable patt] 4 times, moss st 7. *This row sets the position of patt.* Cont in patt. AT THE SAME TIME, shape sides by inc 1 st at each end of 7th row, then every foll 6th row 13 times, then every foll 8th row 5 times (109 sts). Take extra sts into patt as they occur. Patt one row (126 rows) or until length desired. Cast off.

MAKING UP

Press all pieces, except ribbing, gently on ws using a warm iron over a damp cloth. Using backstitch, join shoulder seams. Center sleeves and join. Join side and sleeve seams using edge-to-edge stitch on ribs.

Neckband Using 4.00mm needles, cast on 17 sts.

Row 1 K1, row 1 cable patt, moss st 7. *This row sets position of patt (note the extra k st before the cable patt is worked as a p st on even rows and is used when sewing band into position).* Work until band is long enough when slightly stretched to fit around neckhole.

Bottom band Work as for neckband, make long enough when slightly stretched to fit around body of garment. With rs facing and cable panel of band closest to seam, pin neckband around neckhole and bottom band around garment. Sew into position. Fold band in half (ws together), and sew moss st edge to inside edge of hem. Press seams.

Child's Sweater

BACK

Using 5.00mm needles, cast on 93 (99) sts.

Row 1 Moss st 2 (5), [row 1 cable patt, moss st 7] 5 times, row 1 cable patt, moss st 2 (5). *This row sets position of patt.*** Cont in patt until row 134 (144) has been completed. Cast off.

FRONT

Work as given for back to **. Cont in patt for 116 (126) rows.

Next row, shape front neck Patt 41 (44) sts, turn, and leave rem sts on a holder. Work each side of neck separately. Cast off 2 sts at neck edge of next 2 rows and 1 st on foll rows 7 times [30 (33) sts]. Patt 8 rows. Cast off. With rs facing, rejoin yarn to rem sts, cast off center 11 sts, patt to end. Complete to match first side rev, all shaping.

SLEEVES

Using 3.25mm needles, cast on 40 sts. Work 19 rows in k1, p1 rib.

Next row (inc) On ws, rib 4 [m1, rib 8] 4 times, m1, rib 4 (45 sts). Change to 5.00mm needles.

Row 1 Moss st 2, [row 1 cable patt, moss st 7] 2 times, row 1 cable patt, moss st 2. *This row sets position of patt.* Cont in patt. AT THE SAME TIME, shape sides by inc 1 st at each end of 9th row, then every foll 6th row 10 (13) times [67 (73) sts] Take extra sts into patt as they occur. Patt another 3 (5) rows [72 (92) rows] or until length desired. Cast off.

MAKING UP

Refer to man's sweater pattern.

Graph continued from p. 104

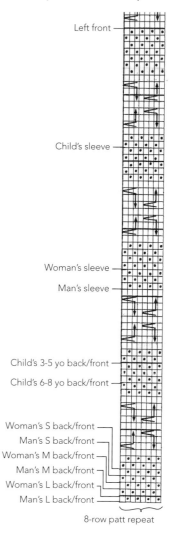

Left front

Child's sleeve

Woman's sleeve
Man's sleeve

Child's 3-5 yo back/front
Child's 6-8 yo back/front

Woman's S back/front
Man's S back/front
Woman's M back/front
Man's M back/front
Woman's L back/front
Man's L back/front

8-row patt repeat

Child's sweater

44 (47) — 24 (30) — 5

45 (48)

3

TRADITIONAL SHAWL COLLAR

WOMAN'S AND MAN'S SWEATER

This garment is suitable for an average knitter. It is a loose-fitting, drop-shouldered sweater with a separately knitted shawl collar.

NEEDLES
- I pair 4.00mm (USA 6) (UK 8)
- I pair 3.25mm (USA 3) (UK 10)
- Cable needle

TENSION
22.5 sts and 30 rows to 10cm, measured over stockinette stitch using 4.00mm needles.

YARN
Jo Sharp 8-ply DK Pure-Wool Handknitting Yarn

	Color	Quantity	
Woman's Sweater	Ginger 322	17	x 50g
Man's Sweater	Antique 323	18	x 50g

BACK
Using 3.25mm needles, cast on 126 sts and rib for 26 rows, as follows:

Row 1 *K4, kb1, p2, rep from * to end.

Row 2 *K2, pb1, p4, rep from * to end.

Row 3 *K4, cr2fk, p1, rep from * to end.

Row 4 *K1, pb1, k1, p4, rep from * to end.

Row 5 *K4, p1, cr2fk, rep from * to end.

Row 6 *Pb1, k2, p4, rep from * to end.

Row 7 *K4, p1, cr2bp, rep from * to end.

Row 8 *k1, pb1, k1, p4, rep from * to end.

Row 9 *K4, cr2bp, p1, rep from * to end.
Rep rows 2 to 9 twice [25 rows].

Row 26 Rep row 2. Change to 4.00mm needles.

Row 1 (inc) On rs, k15, m1, [k12, m1] 8 times, k15 [135 sts]. Cont in st st until row 81 is completed. **

Refer to graph Foll graph on p. 108 until 196 rows are completed.

Shoulder shaping Cast off 9 sts at beg of next 10 rows. Cast off rem 45 sts.

FRONT
Work as for back until **.

Refer to graph Foll graph on p. 109 until 136 rows are completed.

BACK

Shape front neck Patt 64 sts, turn, and leave rem sts on a holder. Work each side of neck separately. Patt 1 row. Dec 1 st at neck edge on foll rows 3 times [61 sts]. Cont without further shaping for 23 rows. Dec 1 st at neck edge in next and alt rows 6 times, then every 4th row 5 times [50 sts]. Work 1 row.

Shape shoulders Cast off 9 sts at beg of next and foll alt rows 5 times. Cast off rem 5 sts. With rs facing, rejoin yarn at neck edge. Cast off 7 sts, patt to end. Complete second side to match first side, rev all shaping.

SLEEVES
Man's size shown in ( ).
Using 3.25mm needles, cast on 70 (77) sts. Rib for 26 rows, as for back. Change to 4.00mm needles, and cont in st st [refer to sleeve graph on p. 109 from row 34 (64) for patt]. AT THE SAME TIME, shape sides by inc 1 st at each end of 5 (9)th row and foll 4 (6)th row until there are 116 (117) sts. Cont for another 17 rows [110 (140) rows]. Cast off loosely and evenly.

FRONT

- 196
- 190
- 180
- 170
- 160
- 150
- 140
- 130
- 120
- 110
- 100
- 90
- 81

SLEEVE

- 110 (140)
- 100 (130)
- 90 (120)
- 80 (110)
- 70 (100)
- 60 (90)
- 50 (80)
- 40 (70)
- 34 (64)

KEY

☐	K on rs, p on ws
⊡	P on rs, k on ws

COLLAR

Using 3.25mm needles, cast on 16 sts.

Row 1 P1 *p2, k2, rep from * to last 3 sts, p2, k1.

Row 2 P1 *p2, k2, rep from * to last 3 sts, p2, k1. When work measures 8cm, with rs facing, begin shaping left side of work. Inc 1 st at end of next row and foll alt rows 16 times [32 sts]. Cont without further shaping until work measures 46cm from beg. Reverse the shaping back to 16 sts. Cont without further shaping until work measures 67cm. Cast off.

MAKING UP

Press all pieces, except ribbing, gently on ws using a warm iron over a damp cloth. Using backstitch, join shoulder seams. Center sleeves and join. Join side and sleeve seams using edge-to-edge stitch on ribs.

To join collar With rs facing, pin shaped edge of collar to neckhole, overlapping B over A at front (see collar diagram at left). Sew into position. Press seams.

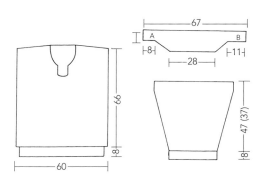

THE CAPE PLAID

WOMAN'S JACKET, MAN'S AND CHILD'S SWEATER

These garments are loose fitting and drop shouldered. The patterns are suitable for an average knitter. The woman's jacket features deep set-in pockets edged with moss stitch and fringe along the sleeve tops. The man's and child's sweaters have a shaped collar with buttoned opening.

NEEDLES

- I pair 3.25mm (USA 3) (UK 10)
- I pair 3.75mm (USA 5) (UK 9)
- I pair 4.00mm (USA 6) (UK 8)

BUTTONS

Woman's jacket—Eight 2.5cm

Man's sweater—Three 1.5cm

Child's sweater—Two 1.5cm

TENSION

22.5 sts and 29 rows to 10cm, measured over patterned stockinette stitch using 4.00mm needles.

YARN

Jo Sharp 8-ply DK Pure-Wool Handknitting Yarn

	Key		Color	Quantity			
				S	(M	L)	
Woman's	1	⊡	Mulberry 325	9	9	10	x 50g
Jacket	2	☐	Jade 316	6	6	6	x 50g
	3	⊞	Lilac 324	2	2	2	x 50g
	4	⊟	Gold 320	1	1	1	x 50g
	5	◪	Antique 323	1	1	1	x 50g
	6	◨	Plum 505	1	1	1	x 50g
Man's	1	⊡	Linen 335	9	9	9	x 50g
Sweater	2	☐	Earth 334	6	6	6	x 50g
	3	⊞	Chestnut 506	2	2	2	x 50g
	4	⊟	Gold 320	1	1	1	x 50g
	5	◪	Antique 323	1	1	1	x 50g
	6	◨	Mosaic 336	1	1	1	x 50g
				3-4	(5-6	7-8) yo	
Child's	1	⊡	Miro 507	5	5	5	x 50g
Sweater	2	☐	Earth 334	3	3	3	x 50g
	3	⊞	Chestnut 506	1	1	1	x 50g
	4	⊟	Gold 320	1	1	1	x 50g
	5	◪	Antique 323	1	1	1	x 50g
	6	◨	Linen 335	1	1	1	x 50g

Woman's Jacket

BACK

Using 3.75mm needles and col 1, cast on 134 (142, 150) sts. Using moss st (*i.e., work in k1, p1 across first row, then in subsequent rows, k all the p sts and p all the k sts as they face you*), work 10 rows. Change to 4.00mm needles. Using st st, beg with a k row, foll graph on pp. 114-115 for 44-row patt repeat for col changes throughout. Work 132 rows. Break yarn, leaving an 8cm end.

Form fringe Cont foll graph on pp. 114-115 for col changes. Using a new piece of yarn of background col for every row, leave 8cm of yarn at each end. Work this way for 66 rows [198 rows]. Cast off.

POCKET LINING (MAKE 2)

Using 4.00mm needles and col 1, cast on 46 sts. Work 50 rows in st st, beg with a k row. Leave sts on a st holder.

LEFT FRONT

Using 3.75mm needles and col 1, cast on 65 (69, 73) sts. Using moss st as for back, work 10 rows. Change to 4.00mm needles. Using st st, beg with a k row, foll graph on pp. 114-115 for 44-row patt repeat for col changes throughout.*

Row 55 (rs)—Place pocket lining Patt 9 (13, 17) sts, slip next 46 sts onto a st holder, and in place of these, patt across 46 sts on first pocket lining, patt 12 (12, 12) sts. Cont in patt until 132 rows are completed. Break yarn, leaving an 8cm end.

Form fringe (left edge) Foll graph on pp. 114-115 for col changes. Using a new piece of yarn of background col for each 2 rows, leave an 8cm yarn end at *beg* of each k row and *end* of each p row. Work this way for 44 rows [176 rows].

BACK, FRONTS & SLEEVES

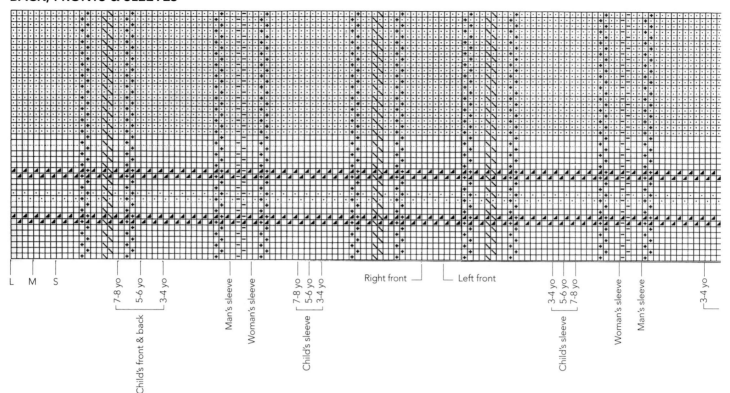

L M S   7-8 yo 5-6 yo 3-4 yo   Man's sleeve Woman's sleeve   7-8 yo 5-6 yo 3-4 yo   Right front ⌐ ⌐ Left front   3-4 yo 5-6 yo 7-8 yo   Woman's sleeve Man's sleeve   3-4 yo

Child's front & back

Child's sleeve

Child's sleeve

Shape front neck Cont foll graph and making fringe as before, work 55 (59, 63) sts, turn, and leave rem 10 sts on a st holder. Cast off 2 sts at beg of next row and foll alt rows twice, and 1 st at neck edge of foll alt rows 3 times [46 (50, 54) sts]. Work 10 rows. Cast off.

RIGHT FRONT

Work as for left front to *.

Row 55 (rs)—Place pocket lining Patt 12 (12, 12) sts, slip next 46 sts onto a st holder, and in place of these, patt across 46 sts of second pocket lining, patt 9 (13, 17) sts. Cont in patt until 133 rows are completed. Break yarn, leaving an 8cm end.

Form fringe (right edge) Foll graph above for col changes. Using a new piece of yarn of background col for each 2 rows, leave an 8cm yarn end at *beg* of each p row and *end* of each k row. Work this way for 44 rows [177 rows].

Shape front neck Cont foll graph and making fringe as before, work 55 (59, 63) sts, turn, and leave rem 10 sts on a st holder. Cast off 2 sts at beg of next row and foll alt rows twice, and 1 st at neck edge of foll alt rows 3 times [46 (50, 54) sts]. Work 9 rows. Cast off.

SLEEVES

Using 3.25mm needles and col 1, cast on 65 sts. Using moss st, work 10 rows. Change to 4.00mm needles. Using st st, beg with a k row, foll graph above for 44-row patt repeat for col changes throughout. AT THE SAME TIME, shape sides by inc 1 st at each end of 7th row and every foll 5th row 19 times (105 sts). Work 4 rows (106 rows). Cast off loosely and evenly.

MAKING UP

Press all pieces, except moss st bands, gently on ws using a warm iron over a damp cloth. Using backstitch, join shoulder seams. Center sleeves and join. Join side and sleeve seams.

Button band Using 3.75mm needles and col 1, cast on 8 sts. Work in moss st until band is long enough when slightly stretched to fit from bottom edge of front to beg of neck shaping. Sew band into position as you go. Leave the 8 sts on the st holder at neckline. Place markers on band for 7 buttons, the first to be placed 2cm from cast-on edge, the 7th at top of band, and the other 5 spaced evenly between.

Buttonhole band Work as for button band, making buttonholes to correspond with position of markers as follows: With rs facing, moss st 2, cast off 3, moss st 3. On next row, cast on 3 sts in place of those cast off on previous row.

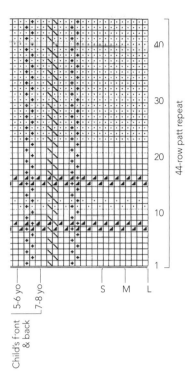

Woman's jacket

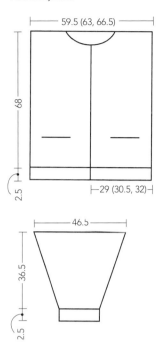

Collar With rs facing, using 3.75mm needles and col 1, pick up 18 sts from st holder at neckline; 26 sts up right front neck; 44 sts from back neck; 26 sts down left front neck; and 18 sts from st holder at left front neck (132 sts). Using moss st, work 19 rows. Change to 4.00mm needles, and cont in moss st until collar measures 11cm at center back, making 1 more buttonhole, evenly spaced from 7th buttonhole. Cast off loosely and evenly.

Pocket tops With rs facing, using 3.75mm needles and col 1, knit 1 row across sts left on st holder. Change to 3.25mm needles. Using moss st, work 3 rows. Cast off. Sew pocket linings into place on ws, and finish off pocket tops on rs. Sew on buttons. Press seams.

Man's Sweater

BACK
Using 3.75mm needles and col 1, cast on 134 (142, 150) sts. Work in k1, p1 rib for 20 rows. Change to 4.00mm needles. Cont in st st, beg with a k row, foll graph on pp. 114-115 for col changes throughout.* Work 184 rows.

Shape shoulders Cast off 11 (11, 11) sts at beg of next 2 rows, then 9 (10, 11) sts at beg of foll rows 8 times. Leave rem 40 sts on a st holder.

FRONT
Work as given for back to *. Work 132 rows.

Divide for neck Work 64 (68, 72) sts, turn, and leave rem sts on a st holder. Keeping patt correct, cont these sts for 40 rows [173 rows].

Shape front neck With ws facing, cast off 5 sts at beg of next row, 4 sts at beg of foll alt row, and 2 sts on foll alt rows 4 times [47 (51, 55) sts].

Shape shoulders Cast off 11 (11, 11) sts at beg of next row, then 9 (10, 11) sts at beg of foll alt rows 4 times. Slip center 6 sts onto a st holder. Rejoin yarn at neck edge [64 (68, 72) sts] and work as for left side, rev all shaping.

SLEEVES
Using 3.75mm needles and col 1, cast on 62 sts. Work in k1, p1 rib for 19 rows, ending with a rs row.

Next row (inc)
Rib 6, [m1, rib 5] 10 times, m1, rib 6 [73 sts]. Change to 4.00mm needles and work in st st, foll graph on pp. 114-115 for 44-row patt repeat for col changes throughout. AT THE SAME TIME, shape sides by inc 1 st at each end of 7th row and every foll 6th row 19 times [113 sts]. Work 9 rows [130 rows] or until length desired. Cast off loosely and evenly.

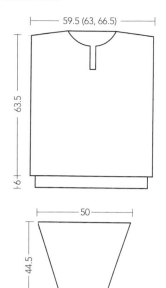

Man's sweater

59.5 (63, 66.5)

63.5

6

50

44.5

6

MAKING UP
Press all pieces, except ribbing, gently on ws using a warm iron over a damp cloth. Using backstitch, join shoulder seams.

Buttonhole band With rs facing, using 3.25mm needles and col 1, place 6 sts from st holder at center front onto left-hand needle and cont as follows:

Row 1 On rs, k2, [p1, k1] into next st, p1, k2 [7 sts].

Row 2 [K1, p1] 3 times, k1.

Row 3 K2, [p1, k1] twice, k1.
Rep rows 2 and 3 throughout. AT THE SAME TIME, make buttonholes at 2cm and 9.5cm from beg as follows:

Buttonhole With rs facing, k2, p1, yon, p2 tog, k2. Cont in rib as set until band is long enough when slightly stretched to fit along neck

opening to beg of neck shaping. Leave sts on a st holder.

Button band Using 3.25mm needles and col 1, cast on 7 sts. Work in rib as for buttonhole band, omitting buttonholes. Sew front bands into place.

Collar With rs facing, using 3.25mm needles and col 1, rib 7 sts from st holder on button band, pick up and k 28 sts up right front neck; 40 sts from st holder back neck; 28 sts down left front neck; and rib 7 sts from st holder on buttonhole band [110 sts]. Work 7 rows k1, p1 rib, dec 1 st at center back neck on first row [109 sts] and working the third buttonhole 17cm from start of buttonhole band.

Shape collar—row 1 K1, *k1, p1, rep from * to last 2 sts, k2.

Row 2 [K1, p1] twice, inc in next st, rib to last 6 sts, inc in next st, rib to end.

Row 3 K2, p1, k1, p2, rib to last 6 sts, p2, k1, p1, k2.

Row 4 Work as row 2.
Rep these 4 rows until collar measures 8cm at center back. Work 2 rows without increasing. Cast off loosely and evenly in rib.
Center sleeves and join. Join side and sleeve seams using edge-to-edge stitch on ribs. Sew on buttons to correspond with buttonholes. Press seams.

Child's Sweater

BACK

Using 3.75mm needles and col 1, cast on 96 (104, 112) sts. Work in k1, p1 rib for 16 rows. Change to 4.00mm needles. Using st st, beg with a k row, foll graph on pp. 114-115 for 44-row patt repeat for col changes throughout.** Work 120 (130, 140) rows. Cast off.

FRONT

Work as given for back to **. Work 80 (90, 100) rows.

Divide for neck Work 45 (49, 53) sts, turn, and leave rem sts on a st holder. Keeping patt correct, cont these sts for 22 rows [103 (113, 123) rows].

Shape front neck With ws facing, cast off 6 sts at beg of next row, 2 sts at beg of foll alt row, and 1 st at neck edge on foll rows 8 times [29 (33, 37) sts]. Work 6 rows [120 (130, 140) rows]. Cast off.
With rs facing, leave 6 sts on a holder, rejoin yarn to rem sts, and complete second side to match first side, rev all shaping.

SLEEVES

Using 3.75mm needles and col 1, cast on 36 (40, 44) sts. Work in k1, p1 rib for 15 rows, ending with a rs row.

Next row (inc) Rib 4 (4, 4), m1, [rib 7 (8, 9), M1] 4 times, rib 4 (4, 4) [41 (45, 49) sts]. Change to 4.00mm needles. Using st st, beg with a k row, foll graph on pp. 114-115 for 44-row patt repeat for col changes throughout. AT THE SAME TIME, shape sides by inc 1 st at each end of 5th row and every foll 4th rows 14 (16, 19) times [71 (79, 89) sts]. Work 9 (7, 5) rows [70 (76, 86) rows]. Cast off loosely and evenly.

MAKING UP

Press all pieces, except ribbing, gently on ws using a warm iron over a damp cloth. Using backstitch, join shoulder seams.

Buttonhole band With rs facing, using 3.25mm needles and col 1, place 6 sts from st holder at center front onto left-hand needle and cont as follows:

Row 1 On rs, k2, [p1, k1] into next st, p1, k2 [7 sts].

Row 2 [K1, p1] 3 times, k1.

Row 3 K2, [p1, k1] twice, k1.
Rep rows 2 and 3 throughout. AT THE SAME TIME, make buttonholes at 1.5cm and 7cm from beg as follows:

Buttonhole With rs facing, k2, p1, yon, p2 tog, k2. Cont in rib as set until band is long enough when slightly stretched to fit along neck opening to beg of neck shaping. Leave sts on a st holder.

Button band
Using 3.25mm needles and col 1, cast on 7 sts. Work in rib as for buttonhole band, omitting buttonholes. Sew front bands into place (buttonhole band on left front for boy and on right front for girl).

Collar With rs facing, using 3.25mm needles and col 1, rib 7 sts from st holder on right front band, pick up and k 26 sts up right side front neck; 38 sts from back neck; 26 sts down left side front neck; and rib 7 sts from st holder on left front band [104 sts].
Work 5 rows k1, p1 rib, dec 1 st at center back neck on first row [103 sts].

Shape collar—row 1 K1, *k1, p1, rep from * to last 2 sts, k2.

Row 2 [K1, p1] twice, inc in next st, rib to last 6 sts, inc in next st, rib to end.

Row 3 K2, p1, k1, p2, rib to last 6 sts, p2, k1, p1, k2.

Row 4 Work as row 2.
Rep these 4 rows until collar measures 6.5cm at center back. Work 2 rows without increasing. Cast off loosely and evenly in rib.
Center sleeves and join. Join side and sleeve seams using edge-to-edge stitch on ribs. Sew on buttons to correspond with buttonholes. Press seams.

Child's sweater

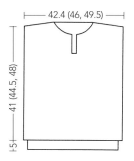

42.4 (46, 49.5)

41 (44.5, 48)

5

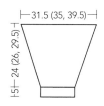

31.5 (35, 39.5)

24 (26, 29.5)

5

5

RIPPLE

WOMAN'S SWEATER

This sweater features raglan-shaped sleeves and a turtleneck collar. The bodice shaping is created using different needle sizes. This pattern is suitable for an average knitter.

NEEDLES
- I pair 3.25mm (USA 3) (UK 10)
- I pair 4.00mm (USA 6) (UK 8)
- Scarf only—crochet hook

TENSION
30 sts and 30 rows to 10cm, measured over patterned stockinette stitch using 4.00mm needles.

STITCH PATTERN
Multiples of 6 + 2

Row 1 On rs, p2, *kbI, kI, pI, kbI, p2, rep from * to end.

Row 2 K2, *pbI, kI, pI, pbI, k2, rep from * to end.

Row 3 P2, *kbI, pI, kI, kbI, p2, rep from * to end.

Row 4 K2, *pbI, pI, kI, pbI, k2, rep from * to end.

Repeat these 4 rows.

YARN
Jo Sharp 8-ply DK Pure-Wool Handknitting Yarn

	Color	Quantity			
		S	(M	L)	
VERSION 1	Natural 301	20	20	21	x 50g
VERSION 2	Citrus 509	20	20	21	x 50g
SCARF	Antique 323	8			x 50g

BACK
Using 3.25mm needles, cast on 158 (170, 182) sts. Using st patt given at left, work 38 rows. Change to 4.00mm needles, and cont in st patt throughout. Work 92 rows (or until length desired) **.

Shape armholes Keeping patt correct, cast off 6 sts at beg of next 2 rows. Dec 1 st at each end of next and foll alt rows 28 (22, 16) times [90 (114, 138) sts], then dec 1 st at each end of every row 14 (26, 38) times [62 sts]. Cast off.

FRONT
Work as given for back to **.

Shape armholes Keeping patt correct, cast off 6 sts at beg of next 2 rows. Dec 1 st at each end of next and foll alt rows 28 (22, 16) times [90 (114, 138) sts], then dec 1 st at each end of every row 1 (13, 25) times.

Next row—shape front neck Keeping patt correct, dec 1 st, patt 20 sts, turn, and leave rem sts on a st holder. Work each side of neck separately. Cont to dec 1 st on each row at sleeve edge. AT THE SAME TIME, dec 1 st on each row at neck edge 8 times (4 sts). Now dec 1 st at sleeve edge of next 3 rows. Cast off. With rs facing, rejoin yarn to rem sts. Cast off next 46 sts. Complete second side to match first side, rev all shaping.

SLEEVES
Using 3.25mm needles, cast on 56 sts. Using st patt, work 36 rows. Change to 4.00mm needles and cont in st patt. AT THE SAME TIME, shape sides by inc 1 st at each end of every alt row 39 times, then every third row 9 times (152 sts). Work 7 rows (adjust length here if desired).

Shape sleeve top Keeping patt correct, cast off 6 sts at beg of next 2 rows. Dec 1 st at each end of next and every alt row 8 times, then 1 st at each end every row 53 times (18 sts). Cast off.

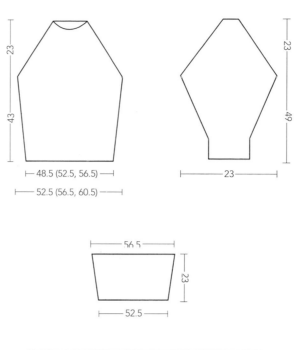

COLLAR

Using 3.25mm needles, cast on 170 sts. Using st patt, work 24 rows. Change to 4.00mm needles, and cont in stitch patt until work measures 23cm. Cast off loosely and evenly.

MAKING UP

Press all pieces gently on ws using a warm iron over a damp cloth. Center sleeves and join to front and back along raglan shaping. Join side and sleeve seams. Using edge-to-edge stitch, join side seams of collar piece. Position collar at center of neckhole with rs of st patt facing inside and seam at the back. Sew collar into place. Press seams.

SCARF

Using 4.00mm needles, cast on 74 sts. Using st patt, work until scarf measures 2 meters (or length desired). Cast off.

Fringe Take four 30cm lengths of yarn and fold in half. Insert crochet hook through the edge of scarf and pull the folded end through, forming a loop. Reach the hook down and draw all the ends through the loop. Pull the ends down to tighten the knot against the edge. Repeat this 18 more times. Repeat on other end of scarf.

RESOURCES

Worldwide

**MAIL-ORDER, RETAIL, AND
WHOLESALE INQUIRIES**

Jo Sharp Handknitting Yarn
P.O. Box 357, Albany, Western Australia 6330
Phone: 800-62-2250;
+61-0898 42 2250
Fax: +61-0898 42 2260
E-mail: josharp@albanyis.com.au
Website: http://www.cybermall.com.au/josharp/

United States

MAIL ORDER

Aussie Connection
135 N.E. Third Ave., Hillsboro, Ore. 97124-3149
Phone: 800-950-2668;
503-693-8441 (international)
E-mail: aussco@teleport.com
Hours: Monday to Friday 8 A.M.-6 P.M. PST;
Saturday 10 A.M.-5 P.M. PST

RETAIL STORES
(*Stores advertising mail-order service)

New Hampshire
The Yarn Express*, 120 Moultonville Rd.,
Center Ossipee 03814 (800-432-1886)

New Jersey
Tomato Factory Yarn Co., 8 Church St.,
Lambertville 08530 (609-397-3475)

Ohio
Abbey Yarns*, 1512 Myers Rd.,
Marion 43302 (800-999-5648)

Oklahoma
Sealed with a Kiss, 1024 E. Noble,
Guthrie 73044 (405-282-8649)

Australia

RETAIL STORES

New South Wales
Craftsmith, Shop 215, Castle Mall,
Castle Hill 2154 (029-680-2241)
Greta's Handcraft Centre, 321 Pacific Highway,
Lindfield 2070 (029-416-2489)
Knit It, Shop 27, Eastwood Village, Progress
Ave., Eastwood 2122 (029-874-1358)
Lady Ann, Shop 7, Sandbank Centre, 65 Victoria
St., Woy Woy 2256 (043-42-2249)
The Wool Inn, Shop 14, NK Centre, 450 High St.,
Penrith 2750 (047-32-2201)
The Wool Shack, Shop 2, Bathurst Plaza,
218 Howich St., Bathurst 2795 (063-32-9223)

Australian Capital Territory
Stitch 'n' Time, Shop 3, Southland,
Mawson 2607 (062-86-4378)

Victoria
Mylady's, 239 Flinders Ln., Melbourne 3000
(039-654-6509)
Purl Plain & Petit Point, 91 Bentinck St.,
Portland 3305 (055-23-6044)
Simply Wool, 189 Yarra St.,
Warrandyte 3113 (039-844-1744)
Warrnambool Wool & Uniform Centre, Lava St.,
Warrnambool 3280 (055-629-599)

Queensland
Miller & Coates, 89 Beatrice St.,
Ascot 4007 (073-268-3955)

South Australia
The Knitting Nook, 16 Adelaide Arcade,
Adelaide 5000 (088-223-4237)

Tasmania
The Needlewoman, 63 Melville St.,
Hobart 7000 (036-234-3966)
The Spinning Wheel, 69 Salamanca Pl.,
Hobart 7000 (036-234-1711)

Western Australia
Crossway's Wool & Fabrics, Crossways S/C,
Rokeby Rd., Subiaco 6008 (089-381-4286)
Greenwood Craft, Shop 5, 95 Wanneroo Rd.,
Greenwood 6024 (089-247-2930)
Hanover Bay Emporium Cnr., Aberdeen St. &
Peels Pl., Albany 6630 (0898-42-1277)

Canada

DISTRIBUTOR

Estelle Designs
Units 65/67 Midland Ave.,
Scarborough, Ont. M1P 3E6
Phone: 416-298-9922

RETAIL STORES

British Columbia
Boutique de Laine, 2530 Estevan Ave.,
Victoria V8R 2S7 (607-592-9616)
Greatest Knits, 1294 Gladstone Ave.,
Victoria V8T 1G6 (604-386-5523)

Manitoba
Ram Wools*, 143 Smith St.,
Winnipeg R3C 1J5 (204-942-2797)
The Sheep Boutique, 153 Evanson St.,
Winnipeg R3G 2A2 (204-786-8887)

Ontario
The Celtic Fox, 1721 Bayview Ave.,
Toronto M4G 3C1 (416-487-8177)
Elizabeth's Wool Shop, 321 Lancaster St. W.,
Kitchener N2H 4V4 (519-744-1881)
The Hill Knittery, 10720 Younge St.,
Richmond Hill L4C 3C9 (905-770-4341)
London Yarns & Machines, 1060 Hyde Park Rd.,
London N0M 1Z0 (519-474-0403)
The Needle Emporium*, 420 Wilson St. E.,
Ancaster L9G 4S4 (905-648-1994; 800-667-9167)
Needles & Knits*, 15040 Younge St.,
Aurora L4G 1N4 (905-713-2066)
Passionknit Ltd.*, 3467 Younge St.,
Toronto M4N 2N3 (416-322-0688)
Rena's Yarns, 6 Sydenham St.,
Dundas L9H 2T4 (905-627-2918)
Romni Wools*, 658 Queen St. W.,
Toronto M6J 1E6 (416-703-0202)
Studio Limestone, 16 Fenwick Ave.,
Toronto M4K 3H3 (416-469-4018)
Village Yarns, 4895 Dundas St. W.,
Toronto M9A 1B2 (416-232-2361)
The Yarn Tree, 34 Thomas St.,
Streetsville L5M 1Y5 (905-821-3170)

Saskatchewan
The Wool Emporium, 7-1501 8th St. E.,
Saskatoon S7H 5J6 (306-374-7848)

PUBLISHER: Suzanne La Rosa
ACQUISITIONS EDITOR: Jolynn Gower
PUBLISHING COORDINATOR: Sarah Coe

EDITOR: Diane Sinitsky
DESIGNER/LAYOUT ARTIST: Amy L. Bernard

TYPEFACES: Centaur, Avenir, Copperplate
PAPER: Patina, 70 lb.
PRINTER: R.R. Donnelly, Willard, Ohio